Let's Eat

Recipes to Fill Your Heart and Home

Mary J. Hubbard

APPETIZERS

"Nor love thy life, nor hate, but while thou livest, live well."

CHEESE TOAST CANAPE Mrs. C. A. Carscadin

Toast small squares or rounds of bread on one side; on the other side grate cheese and set in oven until cheese is melted; add paprika.

CHEESE CANAPES Mrs. E. S. Smith

Cut bread in quarter-inch slices. Spread lightly with French mustard. Sprinkle with grated cheese and finely chopped olives. Brown slightly in oven.

SARDINE AND EGG CANAPE Mrs. C. A. Carscadin

Toast small pieces of bread; cover with a paste made of sardines and a little lemon juice, and top with the yolks of hard boiled egg put through the ricer.

SARDINE CANAPE Mrs. J. A. Kaerwer

Two cans small sardines; one teaspoonful catsup; one teaspoonful lemon juice; a dash of tabasco sauce. Place slice of bread on leaf of lettuce then lay two small sardines across with chopped eggs, and last add catsup, lemon juice and tabasco sauce.

SARDINE CANAPE Mrs. J. A. Kaerwer

Two cans of sardines boned; two tablespoonfuls chopped pickled beets; mix thoroughly and spread on slices of bread; sprinkle chopped eggs over same and serve.

SARDINE CANAPE Mrs. A. D. Campbell

Mash sardines with silver fork, after removing tails and loose skin. Cover with juice of one-half lemon. Spread on thin slices of bread, cut either round or oblong. Cover with grated cheese and toast until cheese melts. Serve hot.

SALMON AND TOMATO CANAPE Mrs. C. A. Carscadin

On a small piece of toast put a paste of salmon, and on this a slice of ripe tomato with mayonnaise.

LOBSTER CANAPE Mrs. Louis Geyler

Chop one-half cup of lobster meat fine and mix thoroughly with the white of two hard boiled eggs which has been pressed through a ricer. Season with salt, pepper, one teaspoonful mustard and moisten with thick mayonnaise. Saute circular pieces of bread until brown, then spread with the mixture. Sprinkle over the top a thin layer of hard boiled yolks and lobster pressed through the ricer.

CANAPES Mrs. Louis Geyler

Dip edges of toast in egg, then in finely minced parsley or chervil; spread with anchovy butter and garnish with cold boiled eggs, olives and capers; or

On the same foundation use tartar sauce, boned anchovies curled around edge and garnish with a stuffed olive or gherkin fan; a gherkin fan is made by cutting it in thin slices, not quite through, and putting the ends together; or

Cover toast with tomato slices, curl anchovy in center and season with lemon, onion juice and paprika; or

Garnish with powdered egg yolk and diced whites; or

Spread toast with anchovy butter, cover with mayonnaise mixed with chili sauce.

MUSHROOM CANAPE (Hot) Miss Agnes Sieber

Cook fresh mushrooms in butter, place on rounds of toast, spread with chervil or parsley butter; pipe a mound of beaten egg white, seasoned with salt and pepper, on each mushroom and place in hot oven until maringue is brown.

PRUNE AND BACON CANAPE (Hot) Miss Agnes Sieber

Remove stones from large prunes and olives; stuff olives with capers and bits of anchovy; put them in the prunes, wrap each prune with bacon and tie with a thread. Place in hot oven until bacon is crisp, remove thread and place on disks of toast spread with Parmesan butter.

TONGUE CANAPE Mrs. F. A. Sieber

Spread toast with mustard cream, garnish with tiny strips of tongue, put a lozenge of white meat of chicken in center, on this put a slice of truffle, both marinated in French dressing.

CANAPE A LA VANDERBILT Mrs. Paul Klein-exel.

Slice of tomatoes on lettuce; combination of crabmeat, celery and pearl onions. Serve with oil mayonnaise.

TUNNYFISH CANAPE Mrs. F. A. Sieber

Spread toast with horseradish butter, lay on strips of tunnyfish and garnish with slices of gherkin.

TOMATO CANAPE Elizabeth Jennings

Lightly toast circles of bread, cut out with biscuit cutter, one-half inch thick. Cover each circle with a slice of tomato. Sprinkle with salt and pepper. Cover tomato with layer of caviar, garnishing edge with finely cut white of hard boiled egg. Instead of caviar, the tiny white onions (bottled) or yolk of egg finely chopped may be substituted. Serve on plate with fancy paper doily.

ANCHOVY PASTE CANAPE Mrs. Paul Klein-exel.

Slice of toast, cut shape of tomato; spread with anchovy paste; topped with tomato slice, and yellow American cheese, browned and melted in oven. Toast only one side of bread.

SARDINOLA CANAPE Mrs. Frederick T. Hoyt

Cut rounds of fresh bread and toast lightly in oven. Cover with Sardinola paste, then sprinkle grated cheese over top, then brown slightly and serve while hot.

CHICKEN, HAM OR TONGUE CANAPES Mrs. Louis Geyler

Spread toast with mustard butter, cover with minced chicken and garnish with olives, pickles, capers and pearl onions; or

Border edge of toast with minced tongue or ham, fill center with chicken mixed with mayonnaise and garnish with minced truffles.

ANCHOVIES AND TOMATOES

Cover anchovies with lemon juice and paprika; in an hour or two place them on tomato slices sprinkled with pulverized egg yolk and garnish with the egg white cut in strips.

ARTICHOKE FONDS OR CELERY CUPS

Parboil six artichokes, or celery hearts cut in cups, in salted acidulated water, cool and marinate in French dressing; fill cups with diced or shredded mixed vegetables and top with mayonnaise; or

Coat the cups with aspic and fill with caviar.

Canned artichokes which are already cooked may be used.

CUCUMBER CROWNS

Cut peeled cucumbers into inch lengths, scoop out centers, leaving a little at the bottom, fill with lobster or shrimp cream and garnish edge with anchovies, mixed olives, capers or pimentoes; or

Fill with caviar mixed with lemon juice and garnish with pearl onions and minced cress.

SHRIMPS AND EGGS

Cut hard boiled eggs in halves, remove yolks and fill with shredded shrimps mixed with mayonnaise; garnish with powdered yolks and serve on lettuce leaves.

EASTER APPETIZER Mrs. A. J. Atwater

Hard boil as many eggs as you have services; peel and cut the whites to represent baskets, carefully scoop out the yolks and fill the baskets with caviar. Toast rounds of bread, cover with the yolks which have been put through ricer, stand a basket in the center of each and serve with a thin slice of lemon.

SWEETBREAD CANAPE Mrs. Louis Geyler

Spread brown bread toast with creamed butter mixed with pate de foie gras; cover with cooked sweetbreads mixed with cucumber, pepper, gras and mayonnaise. Garnish with sweet red peppers.

CANAPE Mrs. W. D. Hurlbut

Spread rounds of toast with liver sausage; garnish with yolks of hard boiled egg put through ricer; in the center place a spoonful of minced stuffed olives.

SARDINE CANAPE Mrs. J. G. Sherer

Spread rounds of toast with mayonnaise; cover with a slice of tomato; mince sardines with yolk of a hard boiled egg and finely chopped stuffed olives; cover the tomato with this mixture and place a spoonful of mayonnaise on top.

CRAB FLAKE CANAPE Mrs. J. G. Sherer

Rounds of bread toasted on one side; spread untoasted side with a mixture of butter and Parmesan cheese. To a small quantity of cream sauce, add one cup crab flakes and heat. Put mounds of crab flakes on the buttered toast and put under blaze long enough to brown slightly.

SAUSAGE AND OLIVE CANAPE Mrs. P. D. Swigart

Toast rounds of bread on one side; spread the untoasted side with mayonnaise, and on this lay a slice of summer sausage as thin as it can be cut; top with minced olive and pimento in mayonnaise.

OLIVE AND NUT CANAPE Mrs. H. Clay Calhoun

To one cup minced stuffed olives add one-half cup minced nut meats and one-half cup oil mayonnaise; mix well and spread on toasted bread cut in any shape you want. Garnish with a little mound of mayonnaise sprinkled with paprika.

FRUIT COCKTAIL Mrs. W. D. Hurlbut

Shred some pineapple; add grape fruit pulp and seeded white grapes; cover with hot sugar and water syrup and let stand until cold; flavor with sherry and serve in cocktail glasses that have been chilled by filling with ice an hour before time to serve.

FRUIT COCKTAIL Mrs. A. Donald Campbell

Scoop out rounds of watermelon and cantaloupe, thoroughly chilled; put in glasses, sprinkle with pulverized sugar and pour over each two tablespoonfuls ice cold ginger ale. Garnish with cherry.

STRAWBERRY COCKTAIL Mrs. H. W. Keil

Select large ripe berries, and if very sandy, wash them. Remove hulls and cut them in halves lengthwise; fill glasses with berries and pour over them a dressing made by mixing one cup of water and two tablespoonfuls sugar, let boil three minutes; cool and add one-half cup claret; let this dressing be ice cold when poured over the berries. Serve.

CHERRY COCKTAIL Mrs. J. G. Sherer

Select the big California cherries; take out the stones and insert in their places walnut, almond or hazel nut meats. Half fill the glasses with a cold syrup made of fruit juice and a little sugar.

ORANGE COCKTAIL Mrs. H. F. Vehmeyer

Remove the skin from the orange sections, place in a chilled cocktail glass and pour over a syrup made of sweetened orange juice and a little sherry. Decorate with sugar coated mint sprays.

TOMATO COCKTAIL Mrs. Magda West

Select uniform sized tomatoes; cut in halves lengthwise. In each glass place a small, crisp leaf of head lettuce; put one-half of a tomato on each and half fill the glass with cocktail sauce.

SHRIMP COCKTAIL Mrs. A. M. Cameron

Boil green shrimp until tender, about twenty-five minutes. Peel and break in halves, if large; dice celery and olives with the shrimp, mix well and cover with a cocktail sauce.

SARDINE COCKTAIL Mrs. W. D. Hurlbut

Drain sardines from oil in box; remove skin, tail and bones; break into small pieces; mince celery and mix with it; put in cocktail glass and cover with sauce made of one-half cup catsup, juice of one lemon; tablespoonful horseradish and a little salt.

CRABMEAT COCKTAIL Mrs. C. A. Carscadin

Two tablespoonfuls crabmeat to each person. To one cup tomato catsup add juice of one lemon, two tablespoonfuls grated horseradish thinned with vinegar; a few drops of tabasco sauce and just before serving, a tablespoonful cracked ice.

CRAB FLAKE COCKTAIL Mrs. J. G. Sherer

To one cup of Japanese crab flakes mince one stalk of celery, one teaspoonful capers and mix well. Fill green pepper cases with the mixture and cover with two tablespoonfuls cocktail sauce.

CLAM COCKTAIL SAUCE

Three tablespoonfuls of tomato, or mushroom catsup; three tablespoonfuls lemon juice; one tablespoonful horseradish; a few drops tabasco; salt and paprika. Stir well and allow about two tablespoonfuls of the sauce for each cocktail.

COCKTAIL SAUCE

Mix well four tablespoonfuls tomato catsup; one of vinegar; two of lemon juice; one of grated horseradish; one of Worcestershire sauce; one teaspoonful salt and a few drops of tabasco. Have very cold when poured over cocktails.

COCKTAIL SAUCE Mrs. W. L. Gregson

One tablespoonful freshly grated horseradish; one tablespoonful vinegar; half a teaspoonful tabasco sauce; two tablespoonfuls lemon juice; one tablespoonful chili sauce; half a teaspoonful Worcestershire sauce. Mix and let stand on ice until ready to serve.

COCKTAIL SAUCE

Two tablespoonfuls each tomato catsup and sherry wine; one tablespoonful lemon juice; a few drops tabasco sauce; half a teaspoonful minced chives and a little salt. Have thoroughly chilled before pouring over cocktail.

COCKTAIL SAUCE

Rub a bowl with a clove of garlic; two tablespoonfuls tomato catsup; one tablespoonful grated horseradish; one tablespoonful mushroom catsup; one teaspoonful lemon juice; one teaspoonful finely chopped chives; a few drops of tabasco sauce, salt and pepper.

SOUPS

All human history attests:
That happiness for man—the hungry sinner—
Since Eve ate apples—much depends on
dinner.
—Byron.

CREAM OF ASPARAGUS Mrs. K. T. Cary

Cook one bunch of asparagus twenty minutes, drain and reserve tops; add two cups of stock and one slice of onion minced; boil thirty minutes. Rub through sieve and thicken with two tablespoonfuls butter and two tablespoonfuls of flour rubbed together. Add salt, pepper, two cups milk and the tips.

CREAM OF BEAN SOUP Mrs. E. D. Kenfield

Put one quart of milk to heat. While it is heating, put the cooked beans through colander. Blend one tablespoonful butter with one of flour; pour over this the hot milk. Season with salt and pepper, stir until smooth, and then add the beans. Pea or asparagus soup can be made in the same way.

CREAM OF CABBAGE

Cut up one small head of cabbage and boil until quite tender. Put it through a colander, add one quart of milk, salt and pepper and thicken with two tablespoonfuls each of butter and flour rubbed together.

CREAM OF CELERY Mrs. W. D. Hurlbut

Cut four heads celery into small pieces and boil it in three pints of water with one-fourth pound of lean ham minced; simmer gently for an hour. Strain through a sieve and return to the pan adding one quart of milk, salt and pepper; thicken with two tablespoonfuls of butter and two tablespoonfuls of flour rubbed to a paste. Serve with whipped cream on top.

CREAM OF CORN Mrs. A. Donald Campbell

Put one can of corn on to simmer with one pint of water and one small onion sliced; cook thirty minutes. Strain, return to the pan, adding one quart of milk, salt and pepper and thicken with two tablespoonfuls of flour and butter. Serve hot with a spoonful of whipped cream on top.

CREAM OF LIMA BEANS Mrs. A. J. Atwater

If dried beans are used, soak them over night; in the morning drain and add three pints of cold water; cook until soft and run through a sieve. Slice two onions and a carrot and cook in two tablespoonfuls of butter; remove vegetables, add two tablespoonfuls flour, salt and pepper, stirring until very smooth; add to this one cup of milk or cream and put into the strained soup; reheat and add two tablespoonfuls more of butter in small pieces.

CREAM OF MUSHROOM SOUP Mrs. J. H. Harris

One-half pound of mushrooms, cleaned and chopped fine, add to four cups of chicken broth, cook twenty minutes; thicken with two tablespoonfuls butter and two of flour blended with one cup of boiling water. When the boiling point is reached add one cup of cream and the well beaten yolks of two eggs.

MUSHROOM SOUP Mrs. Harry Freeman

One-half pound mushrooms, washed and peeled and chopped very fine; cover with one pint of water and boil one-half hour slowly; one quart milk scald in double boiler; season with one tablespoonful butter, salt and pepper; add mushrooms and let come to a boil. Just before serving, add finely chopped parsley. Thicken milk with one tablespoonful flour mixed with cold water and put through a strainer.

CREAM OF RICE SOUP Mrs. W. I. Clock

One cup rice; one large onion; one quart milk; one tablespoonful butter. Boil rice in salted water until tender, press through sieve, and add milk slowly, stirring constantly until all is well mixed, lastly add butter and season to taste.

CREAM OF SPINACH

Wash and cook enough spinach to make a pint; chop it fine and put in a pan with two tablespoonfuls of butter, one teaspoonful salt and a few gratings of nutmeg; cook and stir it about ten minutes; add three pints of soup stock, let it boil up and put it through a strainer. Set it on the fire again and when at the boiling point remove and add one tablespoonful of butter and one teaspoonful of sugar. Thicken with flour mixed with milk or water.

CREAM OF TOMATO

Cook one quart of tomatoes with one slice onion, two teaspoonfuls sugar and one-fourth teaspoonful soda about fifteen minutes; rub through a sieve and set to one side. Scald one quart of milk and thicken with flour diluted with cold water; be careful that the mixture is free from lumps; cook from fifteen to twenty minutes; when ready to serve combine the mixtures, add bits of butter, salt and pepper and a spoonful of whipped cream on top.

CHOWDER Mrs. C. A. Carscadin

One can of corn; one cupful of diced potatoes; one and one-half inch cube of fat salt pork; one tablespoonful onion juice; four cupfuls of scalded milk; two tablespoonfuls of butter; a teaspoonful of salt and a teaspoonful of pepper. Cut pork into small bits and fry until nicely browned; add onion juice and milk and potatoes, which have been boiled in salted water until tender; corn, salt and pepper. Let all just come to the boiling point. Put a few rolled crackers in each plate and pour in chowder. Tomatoes may be added if liked.

CLAM SOUP

Chop fine 25 clams. Put over the fire the liquor that was drained from them and a cup of water; add the chopped clams and boil half an hour; season to taste with salt, pepper and butter; boil up again and add one quart of milk, boiling hot, and two crackers which have been rolled fine. Serve.

MOCK CHICKEN SOUP L. E. Kennedy

Two tablespoonfuls flour; one and one-half pints beef stock; two tablespoonfuls cream; one egg; butter size of an egg. Put butter and flour in a saucepan, stir until smooth; add stock little by little; just before taking from the fire add the cream and egg well beaten together. Salt and pepper to taste.

COURT BOUILLON Mrs. Robert Woods

Take six nice slices of red fish, roll them in flour, season with salt and fry in hot lard, but not entirely done, simply brown on both sides, and set aside. For the sauce, fry in hot lard a large onion chopped fine and a spoonful of flour. When brown, stir in a wineglass of claret, large spoonfuls of garlic and parsley chopped fine, three bay leaves, a spray of thyme, a piece of strong red pepper and salt to taste. Lastly, add your fried fish and cook slowly for an hour. Serve with toast bread.

TOMATO BOUILLON Clara L. Scott

Four cups tomato; four stalks celery; one small onion; four cups water; sugar, salt and pepper to taste; boil until celery is well done. Strain and serve in cups with whipped cream.

VEGETABLE BOUILLON Mrs. W. L. Gregson

Two tablespoonfuls of sugar; one carrot; one onion; one pint tomatoes; three stalks celery (or salt spoon of celery seed); two whole cloves; one salt spoon pepper; one bay leaf; blade of mace; one teaspoonful salt; two quarts cold water; white of one egg; small piece of butter. Burn sugar in kettle, add onion and brown; add carrot and celery, and then cold water and other ingredients except butter and egg. Mix thoroughly, boil, strain through two thicknesses of cheese-cloth, add butter and serve.

JELLIED TOMATO BOUILLON Mrs. P. J. Lanten

Put one quart of tomatoes in pan and simmer twenty minutes; add one-third package of gelatine and stir until dissolved. Strain through a fine sieve, season with salt, pepper and put in ice box to harden. Cut in cubes in bouillon cups and serve with thin slices of lemon.

CREOLE GUMBO Mrs. Robert Woods

Clean a nice young chicken, cut in pieces and fry in hot lard. Add a large sliced onion, a spoonful of flour, two dozen boiled shrimps, two dozen oysters and a few pieces of ham. Fry all together and when brown add a quart and a half of water, and let boil for an hour. Season with chopped parsley, salt and strong pepper. Just before removing and while boiling, stir in quickly a teaspoonful of the powdered file. Take away and pour in tureen. Serve hot with rice cooked dry.

CREOLE GUMBO No. 2 Mrs. Robert Woods

Cut an old fat chicken into small pieces, chop small four onions, place the onions in five ounces of lard and let cook until well browned. Then put in four spoonfuls of flour and let cook five minutes. Put in half gallon good rich stock, add a can of tomatoes, can of okra, season with salt, pepper and cayenne. Tie a small quantity of thyme, sweet bay leaves and parsley in a bit of cloth. Then add twenty-four large shrimps, half dozen hard shell crabs and twenty-four oysters. Let the whole cook for two hours on slow fire. Serve with rice boiled dry for each person.

BROWN SOUP Mrs. Joseph T. Bowen

After boiling a soup bone thoroughly, add a can of tomatoes; strain and put it on the stove again; brown flour enough to thicken it to the consistence of cream; add a lemon or two (sliced very thin and boiled a few minutes in water); one teaspoonful each of ground cloves; cinnamon and allspice. Just before you wish to serve add the hard boiled yolk of an egg for each person; chop the whites and put in the tureen.

SPLIT PEA SOUP Mrs. W. D. Hurlbut

Wash well a pint of split peas and cover with cold water, adding one-third teaspoonful of soda; let them remain in this over night to swell. In the morning put them in a kettle with a close fitting top; pour over them three quarts of cold water, adding half a pound of lean ham or bacon cut into slices or pieces; also a teaspoonful salt, a little pepper and a stalk of celery cut fine. When the soup begins to boil, skim the froth from the surface. Cook slowly from three to four hours, stirring occasionally until the peas are all dissolved. Strain through a colander and leave out meat. It should be quite thick. If not rich enough, add a small piece of butter. Serve with small squares of toasted bread cut up and added.

POTATO SOUP Anna Moss

Peel and slice five medium sized potatoes, cook in boiling salted water; when soft put through a strainer. Scald one quart of milk with one small onion sliced, remove onion and add milk slowly to potatoes. Melt three tablespoonfuls butter, add two tablespoonfuls of flour, one teaspoonful salt, one-quarter spoonful celery salt and dash of white pepper and stir until thoroughly mixed, add to the boiling soup; cook one minute, strain and serve; sprinkle with chopped parsley.

MEAT JELLY L. E. Kennedy

Two pounds of lean beef; one-half gallon cold water; six whole cloves; one-half box gelatin soaked in one-half cupful of water for fifteen minutes; six black pepper corns; one tablespoonful salt; two tablespoonfuls sherry; the juice of one lemon. Cut the beef into the water, add peppercorns, cloves and salt and let simmer slowly four hours. Add the gelatin and strain; to this add lemon juice and pour into a mold. When cold it will slice nicely.

RICE AND TOMATO SOUP

Boil to a pulp, in a quart of water, twelve ripe tomatoes which have been peeled and cut up. Strain, place on stove and add two tablespoonfuls butter rubbed into two tablespoonfuls of flour; add salt, pepper and sugar to taste, onion juice and minced parsley. Cook ten minutes and stir in one cup of cooked rice.

ONION SOUP Mrs. E. P. Rowen

Slice and boil until tender eight medium sized onions; have a strong soup stock ready; add the onions and season to taste. In each plate place a piece of toast and grate Parmesan cheese over it, then slowly add the soup the heat of which will melt the cheese. Serve.

OXTAIL SOUP Mrs. H. J. Keil

One nice meaty oxtail; two medium sized carrots; two onions; one small turnip; two-thirds teaspoonful Kitchen Bouquet; one bay leaf; four peppercorns; two or three celery leaves; dash of pepper; salt to taste. Wash and cover oxtail with water, add carrots cut in cubes. Cut onion and turnip fine and put in a muslin bag with bay leaf, peppercorns and celery leaves. This will leave only the carrot and meat in soup for table. Bring to a boil and simmer for about four hours. Add pepper, salt and Kitchen Bouquet and serve.

FISH

"The fish called the flounder, perhaps you may know,
  Has one side for use and another for show;
  One side for the public, a delicate brown,
  And one that is white, which he always keeps down."
—Holmes.

FISH DELIGHT Mrs. William Blanchard

Mix enough uncooked white fish or Halibut to make two cups; add half a cup soft bread crumbs; three-fourths cup cream. Press through a colander, season with salt, pepper, lemon juice, and a little Worcestershire sauce. Fold in carefully beaten whites of the two eggs. Turn into buttered molds and steam one hour. Serve hot with Hollandaise sauce.

STEAMED HALIBUT, LOBSTER SAUCE Mrs. W. R. McGhee

Butter a steamer and place a thick slice of Halibut steak on it; put over hot water and cook until done. Remove to hot platter and pour over it hot lobster sauce.

Lobster Sauce: Remove the meat from a fresh lobster, about one and one-half pounds; make a rich cream sauce, add the lobster and pour over Halibut.

BAKED HALIBUT

One thick slice of Halibut; one small onion; one tablespoonful butter; one saltspoonful pepper; one teaspoonful Kitchen Bouquet; one level teaspoonful salt; one-half cup water. Chop the onion and put in bottom of baking pan. Put Halibut on top and dust with salt and pepper. Pour over the water to which has been added the Kitchen Bouquet, and then add the melted butter. Bake in rather quick oven until nicely browned. Garnish with parsley and slices of lemon and pour over sauce left in pan.

FISH SOUFFLE Mrs. W. I. Clock

One cup baked fish; four eggs; one cup bread crumbs; one heaping tablespoonful butter. Mix flaked fish and fresh bread or crumbs, place in greased baking dish, pour over the beaten eggs and milk; the seasoning should be added to the fish and bread crumbs before placing in dish. Add the butter in small pieces over the top of the dish, before placing in oven. Bake in hot oven thirty minutes.

FISH WITH TOMATO SAUCE Mrs. Robert Woods

Bake a well selected fish in oven after seasoning with pepper and salt. When done serve with sauce made as follows:

Pour a quantity of sweet oil in a saucepan. When hot, add two sliced onions and when they are cooked, add flour and let onions brown in same. Strain a can of tomatoes and add thereto a small glass of good wine, and a box of mushrooms chopped fine. Let sauce cook, after adding a boquet of thyme, sweet bay, cloves, green onions and garlic. Use red pepper only; and pour over baked fish and serve.

CODFISH BALLS Mrs. C. A. Jennings

One and one-half cupfuls of raw codfish picked up; three cupfuls of raw potatoes, diced; one egg; butter size of a walnut; boil potatoes and fish together until potatoes are soft. Mash, and add pepper and a dash of salt, butter and unbeaten egg and beat until light and thoroughly mixed. Shape roughly in a tablespoon and fry in smoking fat.

COD FISH BALLS Belle Shaw

Half pint measure of raw potatoes, cut in small pieces; one-half pint cod, picked to small pieces. Boil together until potatoes are tender; pour off water and mash very fine; add one egg, one tablespoonful cream and dash pepper. Form on a spoon and fry in hot lard. Lay on brown paper to absorb grease. Serve with cream sauce if desired.

Sauce: One tablespoonful butter; one tablespoonful flour; cook but do not brown. Add to this a pint boiling milk, a pinch salt, and a few pieces of cod to flavor.

CODFISH PUFF Mrs. Grant Beebe

Two cups shredded codfish; one cup milk; one tablespoonful flour for thickening; three eggs. Put milk on stove to warm, then add thickening, then codfish that has been soaked and drained, then the beaten yolks. Lastly fold in the whites beaten.

BROILED FINNAN HADDIE Mrs. W. D. Hurlbut

Wash fish well; lay in dripping pan, cover with fresh water and allow to stand an hour. Drain, place on fish plank, brush with melted butter and put under blaze, not too close, and broil for twenty minutes, or until a nice brown. Take out plank, surround the edge with mashed potatoes, decorate with hard boiled eggs and sprigs of parsley.

FRIED SHAD ROE Mrs. W. R. McGhee

Boil shad roe for fifteen minutes in acidulated salted water; remove, cover with cold water and let stand for a few minutes; dry thoroughly and roll in cracker crumbs, egg and again in crumbs and fry. Garnish with lemon slices.

STUFFING FOR FISH Mrs. Max Mauermann

One cup cracker crumbs; one saltspoon salt; one saltspoon pepper; one saltspoon chopped onions; one saltspoon parsley; one teaspoonful capers; one teaspoonful chopped pickles; small piece of butter.

SHAD ROE, BAKED—CASSEROLE Mrs. Louis Geyler

Boil roe in salted water (acidulated) five minutes, drain, and cover with cold water five minutes; drain and wipe dry. Brush with melted butter, dust with salt and pepper and paprika. Put in casserole, pour on one-half cup stock and one-fourth cup best sherry or water and bake twenty minutes. Add to sauce two or three yolks mixed with one cup cream and strain over roe. Or pour over thin tomato sauce.

FROGS LEGS A LA POULETTE Mrs. W. D. Hurlbut

Trim and clean the frogs legs; boil three minutes. Cover with a sauce made as follows: Three tablespoonfuls butter and three of flour rubbed together; add one-half cup of cream and one cup of chicken stock; season with salt and pepper and just before serving add the yolks of two eggs, well beaten, and one-half tablespoonful lemon juice. Very nice served in a chafing dish.

FROGS LEGS, TARTARE SAUCE

Trim and wipe the desired number of frogs legs; sprinkle with salt and pepper, dip in fine cracker crumbs, beaten egg and again in crumbs. Fry three minutes in deep hot fat. Drain and serve at once with tartare sauce.

SALMON EN CASSEROLE Mrs. George D. Milligan

One pint milk; three tablespoonfuls flour; stir until smooth; cook and remove from fire; add one-half cup butter. When cool add two well beaten eggs, pepper and salt and bake in casserole, putting a layer of sauce, then salmon and finish with bread crumbs on top. Bake about thirty minutes.

MOULDED SALMON Mrs. C. A. Robinson

One can of salmon; three eggs; one-half pint milk; chopped parsley, pepper and salt and a little Worcestershire sauce. Chop the salmon very fine, first picking away all skin and bone; beat the eggs, add the seasoning, mix thoroughly and steam two hours in a mould.

SALMON CROQUETTES Mrs. George Longwell

One pound of salmon; one cup cream; two tablespoonfuls butter; one tablespoonful flour; three eggs, seasoning. Chop the salmon fine, make a cream sauce of the butter, flour and cream; add the salmon and seasoning; boil one minute; stir in one well beaten egg and remove from fire. When cold, make into croquettes; dip in cracker crumbs, then in beaten eggs, again in cracker crumbs and fry in deep fat.

COLD SALMON LOAF Mrs. R. E. P. Kline

One pound can of salmon; one-half tablespoonful each of sugar and flour; one tablespoonful melted butter; one teaspoonful salt; one-half teaspoonful mustard; dash of cayenne; yolks of two eggs, beaten; three-fourths cup milk or cream; one-fourth cup vinegar. Pick salmon over and put with other ingredients (after carefully blending them) into double boiler; cook until eggs are done; remove from fire and add three tablespoonfuls of gelatin, softened in cold water. Mould, chill, and serve with cucumber sauce.

Sauce: One-half cup cream, beaten; season with salt, pepper and a little onion juice. Add two tablespoonfuls vinegar and one cucumber chopped fine and drained as dry as possible.

SALMON EN SURPRISE Mrs. T. D. McMicken

Moisten one cup flaked salmon with butter sauce, pinch minced parsley; one hard boiled egg, chopped fine. Line individual buttered molds with mashed potatoes. Fill centers with fish, cover with potato. Turn out carefully, roll in egg crumbs and fry brown. Garnish with a slice of hard boiled egg on top of mold and parsley.

SHELL FISH

*"I wiped away the weeds and foam,
I fetched my sea-born treasures home."*

OYSTER SAUSAGE Mrs. W. L. Gregson

One-half pound of veal; one pint oysters; one-fourth pound of suet; all chopped fine. Add enough rolled cracker to make into patties; dip in egg and fry in butter.

OYSTER CROQUETTES Mrs. Frank Maccoy

Two sets of calf brains, stewed in salt water; one quart oysters, stew in their own liquor until they curl, cut in small pieces. Chop brains and mix with oysters; two tablespoonfuls melted butter; a few drops onion juice; four tablespoonfuls bread crumbs; one-half cup cream. If too dry add a little of the oyster juice. Bake in shells.

DEVILED OYSTERS

One pint of oysters, seasoned with salt and pepper, stiffened with cracker dust to hold shape, place in oyster shells, pour over melted butter. Put shells in a dripping pan and bake in a quick oven to a light brown.

CREAMED OYSTERS IN CHAFING DISH Mrs. Marquis Regan

Put large tablespoonful of butter in chafing dish, when melted add two tablespoonfuls of sifted flour, mix thoroughly, then add juice strained from one quart of oysters, cook until thickness of cream, constantly stirring, then add oysters, cook until edges curl, season to taste with salt and pepper, serve on toasted crackers.

OYSTERS SCALLOPED WITH CELERY Blanch Ellis Layton

One quart of bulk oysters, one-half dozen stalks of celery, cut into one-half inch pieces. Drain the oysters, reserving the liquor. Cover bottom of baking dish with crumbs of bread or crackers, then a layer of the oysters, with a generous dash of salt and pepper and plenty of butter. Over this put a lawyer of the celery, fill the dish in this way and pour over one cup of the oyster liquor. On top sprinkle a thick layer of the crumbs, adding butter in small pieces. Bake one hour in a moderate oven.

OYSTER PIE

Line a shallow pudding pan with light pastry, put in oysters, milk, butter, salt and pepper, bake in a very quick oven 20 minutes; one pint of oysters, one pint milk, one tablespoonful butter, salt and pepper to taste.

ROAST OYSTERS ON THE HALF SHELL Mrs. W. D. Hurlbut

Scrub the shells of live oysters until free from sand; place in dripping pan in a hot oven and roast until shells open; take off the top shell, being careful not to spill the juice in lower shell; serve in the shell with side dish of melted butter.

PANNED OYSTERS Mrs. H. Clay Calhoun

Clean one pint of oysters and drain from their liquor. Put in a stewpan and cook until oysters are plump and edges begin to curl. Shake pan to prevent oysters from adhering to pan. Season with salt, pepper and two tablespoonfuls butter and put over small slices of toast. Garnish with parsley.

OYSTER FRICASSEE Mrs. Arthur M. Lucius

Clean one pint of oysters, heat oyster liquor to boiling point, strain through double thickness of cheese-cloth; add oysters to liquor and cook until plump. Remove oysters with skimmer and add enough cream to oysters to make one cupful. Melt two tablespoonfuls butter and add two of flour; then pour on gradually the hot liquor; add salt, paprika, one teaspoonful finely minced parsley and one egg slightly beaten. Pour over oysters and serve.

BROILED OYSTERS Mrs. W. D. Hurlbut

Clean oysters and dry on a towel. Dip in butter, then in cracker crumbs seasoned with salt and pepper; place in a buttered wire broiler and broil until juice runs; turn and cook other side. Place on toast, mince celery over the oysters and pour over all a thin cream sauce.

BROILED OYSTERS Mrs. W. K. Mitchell

Select large oysters; wrap a thin slice of bacon around each, fastening with a toothpick; place in a broiler, which in turn is put in a dripping pan to catch the drippings; broil until bacon is brown and crisp, turning to cook other side. Garnish with parsley.

OYSTERS IN BROWN SAUCE

One pint oysters; one-fourth cup butter; one-fourth cup flour; one cupful oyster liquor; one-half cup milk; one teaspoonful Kitchen Bouquet; one-half teaspoonful salt; one-eighth teaspoonful pepper. Parboil and drain the oysters. Brown the butter, add the flour and stir until well blended, add oyster liquor, milk, Kitchen Bouquet, salt, pepper and oysters. Serve in patty cases or ramekins.

CASSEROLE OF OYSTERS Miss Agnes Sieber

Line ramekins or large casserole with minced chicken, seasoned well, and moistened with a little cream. Fill with parboiled oysters cut in pieces, and mushrooms sliced sauted in butter and mixed with the following sauce: Cook three tablespoonfuls salt pork fat with three of flour, add salt, cayenne, nutmeg and parsley; also thyme and mushroom parings. Cook a moment, add one and one-half cups white stock, and simmer one hour, skimming often. Strain, add about one-half cup hot cream or enough to make sauce right consistency. Add four drops lemon juice. Cover with more chicken, sprinkle with buttered crumbs, and brown in oven.

OYSTERS AND MACARONI Mrs. H. Clay Calhoun

Boil macaroni in salted water, drain through a colander. Drain oysters until the liquor is all off. In a casserole put alternate layers of macaroni, oysters and a thick cream sauce, until dish is filled; sprinkle top with grated cheese and bake about half an hour.

OMELETTE AUX HUITRES Mrs. R. Woods

Drain two dozen oysters. Have ready some hot lard and throw them in. Let fry until they begin to curl, then spread over them four well beaten eggs seasoned with salt and pepper and stir all together until done. Serve hot.

FRIED SCALLOPS

Clean one quart of scallops, turn into a saucepan and cook until they begin to shrivel; drain and dry between towels. Roll in fine cracker crumbs seasoned with salt and pepper, dip in egg and again in crumbs and fry in deep fat. Garnish with slices of lemon dipped in parsley.

JAMBALAYA OF RICE AND SHRIMPS Mrs. Robert Woods

Boil two dozen of large shrimps; when cold, peel and set aside. Fry in hot lard a chopped onion and a cupful of rice washed in cold water. Let the onion and rice fry well, add the shrimps, stirring constantly. When browned, add enough water to cover the whole. Season with salt and pepper, a bay leaf, thyme and chopped parsley. Let boil slowly, and add water until the rice is well cooked. When done, let it dry and serve hot.

SHRIMP FRICASSEE Mrs. Ada Woods

Boil the desired quantity of shrimp and set aside. For sauce fry in three tablespoonfuls bacon drippings a large onion, chopped fine; when browned, add three tablespoonfuls flour and blend; add slowly about a quart of water, stirring constantly; when smooth add the shrimp; season with a bay leaf, thyme, a tablespoonful chopped parsley and a clove of garlic, minced. Let cook slowly until ready to serve. Boil rice until dry and creamy and serve with the above.

SHRIMP RAMIKINS Mrs. Max Mauermann

One pint of shrimp; one tablespoonful flour; one tablespoonful butter; one tablespoonful catsup; one tablespoonful cream; one cup hot soup stock; two yolks eggs; salt, cayenne pepper and grated onion. Heat butter, add flour, then other ingredients. Cook until smooth, then add shrimp. Fill the ramikins with mixture and cover with cracker crumbs and butter. Bake six minutes.

SHRIMP WIGGLE Mrs. Willard Brown

Make a rich cream sauce; add one can of shrimp and one can of green peas; allow to cook until all is well heated, serve on toast.

CRAB A LA CREOLE

One can Japanese crab meat; four tablespoonfuls shortening; two green peppers; one large onion; three tomatoes; one cupful milk; two tablespoonfuls flour; one teaspoonful Kitchen Bouquet, one teaspoonful salt, one-fourth teaspoonful pepper. Make a white sauce by melting half the shortening, add flour and when well mixed slowly add milk; stir until creamy, add salt and pepper. In another saucepan melt the other half of shortening, when hot, fry onion and pepper, minced, for ten minutes. Then add tomatoes, cut up, and when tender add Kitchen Bouquet and crab meat and stir slowly into the white sauce. When well mixed, pour over buttered toast and serve.

MEATS AND FOWL

*"Some hae meat and canna eat,
And some wad eat that want it.
But we hae meat and we can eat,
And, so the Lord be thank it."*

BEEFSTEAK ROLL Mrs. J. E. Kelly

Use a large slice of round steak cut one-half inch thick. Make a dressing by mixing together: One cupful grated breadcrumbs, two-thirds teaspoonful salt, one well-beaten egg, one tablespoonful melted butter, one small onion, grated, a few dashes of paprika and a half teaspoonful powdered sweet herbs. Lay the steak on a board, sprinkle with salt and pepper, spread thickly with the dressing and roll up. Wind with soft cord to hold in place. Put three tablespoonfuls of pork fat in a frying pan and when very hot, dredge the roll with flour and brown it quickly on all sides. Place meat in kettle that has a tight fitting cover. Meanwhile, add to the fat in the pan two slices of minced onion, and one tablespoonful flour. Stir until very smooth, pour in a cupful of stock (or hot water) and when the gravy boils, pour over the roll with a pint of strained tomato. Season to taste with salt and pepper, cover the kettle closely and as soon as the contents boil, place where it will simmer for about two hours. When cooked, remove the strings, and serve on a heated platter, with the strained gravy poured over it.

HAMBURGER POT DINNER Mrs. Antonio Sterba

With two pounds hamburger steak, mix well one cup raw rice (wash well); one medium sized onion, chopped; season and make into balls. Line bottom of a pot with small pieces of suet; when this is melted, place meat balls in the pot, cover with water, and cook until rice is about done. Add one can of tomatoes (quart can). A half hour before serving, peel enough medium-sized potatoes to circle the platter to be used. Place these on top of tomatoes. When potatoes are done, arrange them around the outside rim of the platter with the meat balls in the center, and pour over the meat enough gravy for first serving. Remainder of gravy may be used on table in a casserole or gravy dish. Care must be used in measuring the rice—too much will cause the balls to fall to pieces. One advantage of this dish is that it may be prepared the day before, or the morning before serving, with the exception of the potatoes.

CALVES' HEARTS STUFFED AND BRAISED Mrs. W. R. McGhee

Remove veins, arteries, and blood clots, wash, stuff and sew. Sprinkle with salt, pepper, roll in flour and brown richly in hot dripping. Place in Dutch oven or in one of the small vessels in fireless cooker. Half cover with boiling water, surround with six slices carrot, one stalk celery, broken in pieces, one onion sliced, two sprays parsley, a bit of bay leaf, three cloves and one-half teaspoonful peppercorns. Cover closely and bake slowly two or more hours basting often if cooked in Dutch oven. If necessary, add more water. Remove hearts to serving platter, strain and thicken the liquor with flour diluted with water. Season with salt, pepper and one-half teaspoonful Kitchen Bouquet.

LUNCHEON BEEF Mrs. I. A. Wilcox

One cup or more of cold cooked beef chopped; one cup of bread crumbs; season with salt, pepper and butter. Place in baking dish and cover with buttered bread crumbs. Pour milk in dish until you can just see it. Bake in oven till light brown on top. Can use any kind of cold cooked beef, as steak, roast, or boiled beef. If you have a few cold mashed potatoes, put them through ricer on top of meat to form upper crust. Dot with butter and let brown.

POT ROAST Mary S. Vanzwoll

Round steak one and one-half inches thick. Salt and pepper. Pound a cup of flour in, on both sides. Sear both sides in melted fat, and butter. Put in baking dish and cover with water. Cook in oven two and one-half hours.

SPANISH STEAK Mrs. W. H. Hart

One and one-half pounds round steak, ground; one and one-half pounds of pork steak, ground; one heaping cupful bread crumbs; one cupful canned or fresh tomatoes; two green peppers, minced; one-half cupful minced onion; one egg; two teaspoonfuls salt. Mix all together and bake forty-five minutes in flat cake.

BRAISED BEEF Mrs. I. S. Blackwelder

Round steak about three inches thick (about two pounds); place in a hot skillet and turn so that it is seared on both sides, to prevent escape of juices. In a covered baking pan make a bed of chopped vegetables (potatoes, turnips, carrots, onions, etc.); season well. Place upon it the beef with enough water to keep the mess steaming for four hours. Cover tight.

MOTHER'S BEEF LOAF Mrs. F. E. Lyons

Three pounds round steak, ground; three eggs; two-thirds cup cracker crumbs; three teaspoonfuls ground sage; two teaspoonfuls salt; one teaspoonful pepper. Mix together thoroughly and bake in a 5x10-inch bread pan, from one to one and one-half hours.

MEAT PIE

Butter an earthen baking dish and line to the depth of one and one-half inches with hot mashed potatoes, season with finely chopped chives (one tablespoonful to two cups mashed potatoes). Fill center with chopped left-over cold beef, veal or chicken. Moisten with brown or cream sauce, to which add one-half tablespoonful minced parsley and onion juice. Cover with a layer of the potato mixture, make several openings in top of pie and brush top over with beaten egg, diluted with milk. Bake in hot oven until heated through and well browned. Serve hot in baking dish.

BRAISED LARDED LIVER Mrs. W. R. McGhee

Skewer, tie in shape (if necessary) and lard the upper side of calf's liver. Place in a deep pan with remnants of lardoons; season with salt and pepper; dredge with flour. Surround with one-half each carrot, onion, celery, cut in dice; one-half teaspoonful peppercorns, six cloves, bit of bay leaf and two cups brown stock or water. Cover closely and bake slowly two hours, uncover the last twenty minutes of cooking. Remove from pan, serve with the French onions or pour around brown sauce.

HAMBURG STEAK Sue C. Woodman

Mix one egg and a little salt and pepper; make into balls and bake in closed pan quickly.

POT ROAST Mrs. C. S. Junge

Procure a Boston cut of roast of beef; brown a minced onion in skillet with butter and bacon fat; in this brown all sides of the roast. Remove the roast and in the fat stir two tablespoonfuls of flour and fill skillet nearly full of hot water. Season this gravy well with salt, pepper, bay and garlic and pour over roast in casserole. Place a few slices of tomato on top or pour in a cup of strained tomato; place some carrots around the roast and put in cooker for at least four hours.

BRAIN PATTIES Mrs. E. Iglehart

Plunge the calf's brains into boiling water for three minutes, remove from water and pick off the dark muscles, roll into cracker dust or bread crumbs in small patties and drop into hot fat. Salt and pepper.

ROAST BEEF SOUFFLE Mrs. H. S. Hart

One tablespoonful butter melted in sauce pan, one tablespoonful of flour added and well mixed, one cup milk. Chop beef, or any kind of cold meat quite fine and add to milk after it has thickened; salt and pepper to taste. Then stir in the yolks of three eggs, cook slightly, cool, add beaten whites of eggs. Put in greased dish and bake about half an hour. Is nice served with tomato sauce or peas. About one and one-half cups of the chopped meat for the above.

MEAT LOAF Mrs. L. E. Brown

Two pounds of round steak; one pound fresh pork; four tomatoes; three pimentoes; two eggs; four crackers, rolled; salt, pepper and paprika. Mix altogether; bake in bread pan two hours in moderate oven. Sauce: One and one-half tablespoonfuls butter, flour and milk. Season with liquid from meat.

TOUGH STEAKS Mrs. E. S. Smith

Pour a mixture of two tablespoonfuls of vinegar; and one of olive oil over a steak. Let stand several hours before broiling. The result is delicious.

VEAL CROQUETTES Belle Shaw

Two pounds veal, chopped fine; one teaspoonful chopped parsley; two eggs, hard boiled and chopped; salt and pepper, to taste. Soak enough bread crumbs, and add to mixture; form balls. Roll in egg and cracker crumbs and fry in deep fat.

BONED AND STUFFED LEG OF LAMB Mrs. H. L. Baumgardner

Order a leg of lamb boned at the market. Make a stuffing as for chicken. Put in roasting pan with a small sliced onion, one-fourth cup each of turnip and carrot, season with bay leaf and parsley. Add three cupfuls of hot water, salt and pepper. Cook slowly until done. Serve with Currant Jelly Sauce.

Currant Jelly Sauce: To the regular brown gravy you would make with roast, add one-half cupful of currant jelly which has been beaten and a little lemon juice; well stirred together and let all boil a minute or two.

LAMB STEW A LA CREOLE

Wipe three pounds lamb, cut from neck or shoulder. Cut into pieces two inches square. Melt one-fourth cup dripping, add meat and stir and brown evenly. Add two onions, thinly sliced, one sprig parsley, small bit bay leaf, two cloves and one-half teaspoonful peppercorns (tie last three spices in a bit of cheese cloth), and boiling water to nearly cover meat. Simmer slowly until meat is tender (about one and one-half hours). Then add two or three small carrots, scraped and cut in lengthwise pieces, season with salt. Parboil six medium-sized potatoes cut in thick slices five minutes, drain, add to stew; add two cups thick tomato puree and simmer slowly until vegetables are tender. Add more water if necessary. Remove spices, add one cup French peas when heated through, turn into deep, hot platter and sprinkle with chopped parsley.

LAMB HASH WITH GREEN PEPPERS Mrs. W. D. Hurlbut

Mince cold roast lamb in about half inch pieces; add a sweet green pepper, minced (discarding seeds); add the gravy and heat thoroughly. Serve on toast.

RECIPE FOR CORNING BEEF Mrs. W. T. Foster

Five tablespoonfuls of salt; two tablespoonfuls of brown sugar; one-half teaspoonful salt peter, or less; this is for five pounds of beef. Cover with water; leave three or four days and boil in same water.

MOCK TERRAPIN Mrs. W. H. Muschlet

Two cupfuls cold boiled or roast lamb cut into small pieces. Put a tablespoonful of butter into double boiler; when melted add one tablespoonful of flour. Rub smooth; add one pint of milk; stir continuously till it thickens; then set pot back where it won't cook hard, and add one well beaten egg, a tablespoonful minced parsley, a little nutmeg, red pepper, salt to taste, two hard boiled eggs cut (not too fine); then the lamb. Let it keep hot, but not boil, till lamb is thoroughly heated. When serving, add a teaspoonful lemon juice.

VEAL LOAF WITH EGG Mrs. H. B. Rairden

Two and one-half pounds of veal; two pork chops, ground together; three eggs; three rolled crackers; one teaspoonful each salt and pepper. Mix well together. Put half of mixture in a loaf pan, peel six eggs which have been hard boiled, clip off the ends so they fit closely together, and lay them in the center of the loaf; place the balance of the meat about them, fill up pan, packing it solid; put in double baker on top of stove to steam for one and one-half hours, spread butter over top and put in oven to finish baking. In slicing it you get the slice of hard boiled egg in the center.

VEAL LOAF Mrs. A. Donald Campbell

One and one-half pounds of veal and one slice of salt pork, chopped fine. Add two tablespoonfuls of cracker dust; one egg; piece of butter size of an egg; one teaspoonful each of salt and pepper; little grated nutmeg; dash of Worcestershire sauce. Mix well and bake in a loaf shaped pan with cracker crumbs and bits of butter on top. Bake about one and three-quarters hours.

BAKED SPICED HAM, ALABAMA STYLE Mrs. K. T. Cary

Soak a fifteen pound ham in cold water to cover over night. Wash, scrub and trim off inedible parts. Set over a trivet in a boiler and cover with boiling water. Mix four cups brown sugar, one large sliced onion, one red Chili pepper pod, one tablespoonful each of whole cloves, allspice and cassia buds, two thinly sliced lemons, discarding seeds, add to water in boiler. Cover and cook slowly two and one-half hours. Remove from boiler, peel off rind and put ham in dripping pan, fat side up. Bake slowly two and one-half hours, basting with one cup sherry wine (using a tablespoon) a little at a time until all is used, then baste with dripping in pan thirty minutes, before removing from oven, sprinkle fat side with equal measures of brown sugar and fine bread crumbs, stick with cloves and brown richly. Serve hot champagne, horseradish or mustard sauce.

KOLDOLMA Mrs. F. W. Waddell

Two pounds of veal; one pound fresh pork; one-half lemon, bay leaf and one small bottle capers; one clove of garlic; juice of one onion. Put all through grinder, salt, pepper to taste. Roll in small soft balls. Enclose neatly in cabbage leaves, secure with toothpicks. Place in Dutch oven which has previously melted one-fourth pound of butter with a little chopped parsley. Alternate layers with a small sifting of flour until all are in pan. Let simmer in one pint of water (boiling) without allowing any steam to escape for two hours; remove and thicken broth with yolks of five eggs. Serve eight persons.

VIRGINIA HAM Mrs. G. W. Plummer

Buy a center cut of ham, two inches thick (about two and one-half or three pounds); soak over night in milk (sweet or sour) sufficient to cover ham. About two hours before serving time drain off enough milk so that the top of ham is uncovered; spread over this uncovered top; one tablespoonful dry ground mustard mixed with two tablespoonfuls brown sugar; bake in a slow oven. The milk will disappear in a rich brown gravy; if it gets too low in pan add water. When ready to serve remove ham to platter, add flour to fat in pan and when well cooked, add boiling water to make gravy of consistency of thick cream. Lemon slices and sherry may be added. It may need to be strained if milk curds are objected to; pour around ham. Has flavor of finest "Old Virginia Ham."

HAM EN CASSEROLE Mrs. A. Donald Campbell

Have ham cut two inches thick, leaving on rind. Pour over it good, generous cup of milk and one-half cup brown sugar, partly dissolving sugar in the milk on top of stove, before pouring over ham. Cook all in casserole two hours. Serve with rings of fried apples on chop plate.

ROGNONS AUX TOMATOES Mrs. R. Woods

Cut in small pieces a fresh kidney and fry in hot lard. When almost done add to it a sliced onion, half cup of tomatoes and a slice of ham. Let all fry together, and when done add a spoonful of flour, a piece of red pepper and a spoonful of chopped garlic and parsley. Thin with a little water, season with salt, and let boil a few minutes, when it is done.

EASTER HAM Mrs. E. Iglehart

One-half pint grated bread crumbs, one cup currants, one saltspoonful of salt, one saltspoonful sweet marjoram or thyme, one salt spoonful of black pepper, moisten with sweet milk. Boil small ham until tender, remove bone and skin, fill in the cavity with dressing, wind with cord into shape, puncture with skewer in the fat parts and fill the holes with dressing. Bake in a closed pan in a hot oven one hour.

HAM PUFF Mrs. A. Donald Campbell

Scald one pint of milk, one cup flour; stir constantly until thick. Let cool, then add beaten yolks of eight eggs. Beat thoroughly, add beaten whites, a little suet, one and one-half cups of chopped, boiled ham, and one-half cup butter. Set tin in pan of water, and bake three-fourths of an hour. Keep standing in water until served.

HAM LOAF Mrs. W. C. Thorbus

Two pounds of ham, ground; one pound of pork loin, ground; two eggs, beaten; one cupful rolled cracker crumbs; one cupful milk; pepper to taste. Mix all together, put in a baking tin and pour over it one cupful tomatoes and bake two hours.

JAMABALA OF HAM Mrs. H. Clay Calhoun

One large slice of raw ham; one large onion; put through the grinder and fry. When thoroughly cooked add two cups boiled rice; one quart of tomatoes and half of a sweet green pepper, chopped fine. Serve hot on toast.

BARBECUED ROAST PORK Mrs. Chase

Place pork roast in dry self-basting or similar roaster. Place in oven for thirty minutes. In meantime put one cup of vinegar, one teaspoonful red pepper, one teaspoonful black pepper, one teaspoonful salt in saucepan and bring to a boil. Baste roast every fifteen or twenty minutes with this sauce at boiling point, draining off sauce after each basting and returning sauce to saucepan, which should be kept at the boiling point. Drain off sauce and serve in separate dish.

CROWN ROAST OF YOUNG PORK Mrs. M. Dippen

Have crown roast made of young pork ribs, same as of lamb; fill the center with medium sized potatoes, boiled and rolled in butter and minced parsley; surround with fried apples.

BROILED SAUSAGE Mrs. W. D. Hurlbut

One and one-half or two pounds of well seasoned sausage meat mold it into a flat cake; place in a frying basket which, in turn, is put in a larger pan, to catch the drippings. Put under the blaze and let it broil slowly; when nicely browned on one side turn it over and brown that side. When done remove to hot platter and surround with fried apples.

PORK CHOPS WITH POTATOES Mrs. C. S. Junge

In a casserole place a layer of sliced raw potatoes and over it sprinkle of flour. Put in a layer of chops and a layer of potatoes and repeat until casserole is full. Nearly cover with milk that is seasoned with salt and pepper. Sprinkle cheese over top and bake two hours.

GRANDMOTHER'S PORK NOODLES Mrs. H. D. Sheldon

One-half pound of salt pork, sliced; six medium onions; six medium potatoes; noodles. Boil salt pork until very nearly done. Add potatoes and onions. Cook until they are beginning to be tender. Have about two quarts of water left. Add noodles and finish cooking. This will make a thick stew.

PORK CHOP CASSEROLE Mrs. George D. Milligan

Sprinkle bottom of dish with flour; place pork chops then on top a layer of sliced raw potatoes and onions, finish with bread crumbs. Bake until potatoes are done. Use no liquid.

BAKED PORK CHOPS Sue C. Woodman

Cut thick, wash and dip in flour; place in deep pan; season with pepper, salt, and a little sage. Cover tightly and bake forty minutes in quick oven.

STUFFED PORK TENDERLOINS Mrs. C. E. Balluff

Split two large tenderloins and flatten out as wide as possible, spread one with a very thick layer of dressing (such as is used for turkey dressing). Place the second tenderloin on this and tie them together, roast in a medium oven, basting frequently with boiling water and a small piece of melted butter.

STUFFED SPARERIBS Mrs. H. L. Middleton

Have two sets of ribs cracked across the middle; rub the insides with salt, pepper and dredge with flour. Cook sauerkraut half an hour, drain and fill the ribs; tie or sew closely together and put in oven. Pour over the ribs the water in which the sauerkraut was boiled. When one side is browned, turn them over and brown the other side. Serve with brown gravy.

ENGLISH SAUSAGE Mrs. C. A. Carscadin

Six pounds lean pork; two pounds fat pork; one pound loaf bread thoroughly soaked in water; two ounces salt; one ounce best white pepper; two medium sized nutmegs, grated. Mix all together, put into chopper. Leg of pork is best, but shoulder will do.

ESCALLOPED SWEETBREADS Mrs. E. K. Parker

One pair sweetbreads; one can mushrooms; two cups of cream; butter size of an egg; one tablespoonful flour. Parboil sweetbreads twenty minutes then chop rather fine; add mushrooms and chop. Put butter in spider and let it melt and as it begins to brown, add the flour and stir; then add cream, stirring all the time to prevent lumps. Put in the sweetbreads and mushrooms and let cook a few minutes. Add one teaspoonful Worcestershire sauce and pour mixture in baking dish. Put cracker crumbs and lumps of butter on top and bake half an hour.

CREAMED SWEETBREADS WITH TOMATO SAUCE Mrs. W. D. Hurlbut

Parboil sweetbreads in acidulated salt water, cook slowly for twenty minutes; drain, plunge into cold water. Make a rich cream sauce, separate sweetbreads and mix with the cream sauce; put in ramekins, cover with bread crumbs; in the center place a tablespoonful tomato sauce; put in oven and bake until crumbs are brown; place a sprig of parsley on top and serve.

CHICKEN A LA KING Mrs. W. C. Thorbus

Heat two tablespoonfuls butter until it bubbles; add one chopped green pepper; let cook slowly for three minutes, then add one tablespoonful flour; salt and pepper to taste and enough rich milk to make a smooth thickened sauce; when thoroughly done add two cupfuls cooked chicken and let it heat through. Mushrooms may be added.

CHICKEN NOODLES AND MUSHROOMS Mrs. W. D. Hurlbut

Pick the meat from the bones and cut in rather large pieces; add a can of mushrooms and the thickened chicken gravy. Boil noodles twenty minutes in salted water; drain and add noodles to the chicken. Mix all together and let heat thoroughly. Serve with toast points.

CHICKEN A LA CREOLE Mrs. R. Woods

Clean and cut up two young chickens, sprinkle with salt and pepper and fry in hot lard. When done, put in a dish and set aside. And now start your sauce. Fry an onion and add flour for thickening. When brown, add a can of sweet peppers, let fry a little, then add the tomatoes and a few bay leaves and a sprig of thyme. When the sauce is done throw in the fried chickens, but do not let the whole boil long.

SWEET BREAD PATTIES

Parboil one pair sweetbreads in boiling, salted, acidulated water, fifteen minutes. Drain and cut in one-half inch cubes. Add one-half the measure of small mushrooms, heated in the liquor in the can, drained, cooled and sliced, and one tablespoonful pimento cut into bits. Reheat in one and one-half cups of sauce (cream) and serve in patty shells.

BAKED MACARONI AND CHICKEN Bertha Z. Bisbee

Stew until tender a nice fat hen, in plenty of water. Pick meat off bones and shred rather finely. Boil one pound of macaroni or spaghetti twenty minutes in plenty of water to which has been added a teaspoonful of salt. Drain as dry as possible. Cover the bottom of a buttered baking dish with the macaroni, adding chicken and macaroni in alternate layers. Add one cup of cream to the gravy in which the chicken was cooked, salt and pepper to taste, and thicken with flour or corn starch. Pour enough over the macaroni and chicken to cover it. Bake in a slow oven until nicely browned on top.

REAL COTTAGE CHICKEN Mrs. F. W. Waddell

Boil one package of macaroni in salted water in the usual manner. Use three or four pounds chicken. Place in Dutch Oven whole. After browning, four tablespoonfuls of butter with a little parsley cover tightly and simmer forty-five minutes. Remove cover and add salt and pepper. When sufficiently cooked, so that the fowl will slip from the bone, turn out fire and let cool. Remove bones and place in receptacle once more. Add one pint of pure cream, the macaroni previously cooked, and let boil up just three minutes, and let stand until ready to serve. Better to stand for an hour.

BOUCHEES A LA REINE Mrs. Robert Woods

Take good sized young hen and boil it. When done take all the meat, chop it, but not too fine and keep the "bouillon." Have ready some mushrooms and truffles cut in small pieces. Fry an onion in hot lard, add flour and brown well; in this throw your meat, mushrooms and truffles. Give two or three turns in the pan and add the bouillon to make the sauce. Do not make it too thin. Season with a little pepper. The small "pates" are ordered from the confectioner and are kept warm until needed. When the filling is done and you are ready to serve, fill each pate with the stew and send warm to the table.

CHICKEN IN ASPIC Mrs. E. S. Bailey

Draw one large chicken; boil until meat drops from bones and there is about one pint of liquid. Chop chicken and add a teaspoonful of salt and one-half teaspoonful pepper; also one tablespoonful of celery salt. Hard boil three eggs and soak one-half package gelatine five minutes and add to hot liquid. Chill mold and put in layer of chicken and three eggs and put balance of chicken in. Then pour the liquid on mold and chill.

CHICKEN TERRAPIN FOR SIX PEOPLE Mrs. J. P. Cobb

One cup of chicken cut the size of an egg; one cup of canned mushrooms; make a cream sauce of the chicken stock; when this is boiled up, add the chicken and mushrooms, yolk of one egg beaten, one teaspoonful of Worcestershire sauce, teaspoonful sherry. Serve on platter with whipped cream or brown with bread crumbs.

SPANISH CHICKEN Mrs. Lester Tennant

Cut up two chickens, about five pounds in all; good fat yellow hens are the best. Put in a good sized pot and put in cold water enough to cover about two inches over all; cover and let heat very slowly; stew until meat can be picked from the bones. When the liquor the chicken is cooked in becomes cold, remove all fat and save to make stew in. Cut up six fair sized potatoes; one large onion; two large green peppers; one clove of garlic; one can of mushrooms; one can tomatoes; one can of peas; one bottle of little stuffed olives. Remove meat from chicken bones, then put in tomatoes, potatoes, peas, etc., in the liquor. Cut each mushroom through and add one wineglass each of olive oil and good white wine; three fair sized bay leaves; a large pinch of thyme; a few sprigs of parsley; salt; celery salt; black pepper and tobasco sauce to taste. When potatoes are done, add one large tablespoonful butter, put in the chicken meat and the stew is ready to serve. Have plenty of toast to serve chicken on. This will serve sixteen people and may be made the day before.

CURRY OF CHICKEN EN CASSEROLE Mrs. W. P. Hilliard

Clean, singe, dress and cut up a three and one-half pound chicken as for fried chicken; melt one-third cup butter in an iron frying pan; sprinkle chicken with salt and pepper; arrange in hot frying pan and cook ten minutes, turning so as to brown evenly; add giblets; continue cooking ten minutes longer. Arrange chickens in a hot casserole with one thinly sliced onion; one-half tablespoonful salt, and broth or boiling water to cover; cover casserole and simmer in oven until chicken is tender. Remove chicken; strain liquor; melt one-fourth cup butter; add two tablespoonfuls flour, mixed with two tablespoonfuls curry powder; stir until smooth. Add strained liquor (there should be two cups); one-third cup currant jelly and salt to season. Turn one-half of sauce into casserole; arrange chicken over sauce and cover with remaining sauce. Serve in casserole. Serve boiled rice with chicken curry.

SALMI OF DUCK Mrs. S. E. Baumgardner

Cut cold roast duck in pieces and heat in the following sauce: One tablespoonful butter; one small onion chopped fine; a stalk of celery and one sliced carrot; saute until brown then add one tablespoonful flour; two cups water; a bayleaf; a spray of parsley; a few cloves and salt and pepper; let cook a few minutes. Strain, put in the duck; add six olives sliced lengthwise; a small can of mushrooms, cut in two; let all heat and serve.

CREOLE CHICKEN

Cut two chickens in pieces for serving; sprinkle with salt and pepper. Melt one-half cup butter; add one-half cup finely chopped onion; add chickens, saute a golden brown, turning chickens to evenly brown; remove chickens; add one-half cup flour; stir until well blended; then pour on two cups chicken stock and two cups tomato puree; one mild red pepper, finely chopped; one-half can mushrooms, drained and thinly sliced; one cup finely cut celery; season with salt and pepper. Add chickens and simmer until tender. Dispose on hot serving platter; surround with sauce; garnish with parsley.

CHICKEN CURRY WITH MUSHROOMS IN CHAFING DISH Mrs. M. Regan

One medium sized can of boneless chicken; one-half can of French mushrooms; one heaping teaspoonful Indian currypowder; one large tablespoonful of butter; two tablespoonfuls of sifted flour and two cups milk. Put butter in chafing dish, when melted add flour; then milk slowly, and salt and pepper to taste. When creamy add chicken cut fine and chopped mushrooms; stir constantly until heated thoroughly and just before serving add curry powder. Eat on hot toast.

SQUAB EN CASSEROLE Mrs. W. D. Hurlbut

Wash squabs and stuff with boiled rice in which the cooked, minced giblets of the squabs have been mixed; place in casserole and pour a little melted butter over each squab; sprinkle with salt and pepper and onion salt.

Use the water in which the giblets were cooked for stock, there should be one cup. Put in oven and bake until tender.

PIGEON PIE Mrs. Culbertson

Dress, clean and truss six young, fat pigeons. Brown them richly in tried out salt pork fat. Put in a Dutch oven or kettle, cover with boiling water. Add two stalks celery, broken in pieces; a bit of bay leaf; one-half teaspoonful pepper-corns; one onion sliced; six slices of carrot; two sprays parsley and simmer five to six hours or until tender. Add one-half tablespoonful salt last hour of cooking. Remove pigeons; strain liquid and thicken with one-fourth cup butter, cooked one minute with one-fourth cup flour, stirring constantly, until gravy is smooth. Arrange pigeon in a deep baking dish; pour over gravy and cover with a baking powder crust, and bake in a hot oven.

A GOOD IMITATION OF MARYLAND FRIED CHICKEN Mrs. J. G. Sherer

It may be made from rabbit. Choose a young tender rabbit; cut it into pieces of desired size; put pieces in a pot, cover with boiling water, and parboil gently for twenty minutes; dip each piece in flour, egg and cracker crumbs and fry in deep fat until a rich brown. Evaporate by boiling some of the water in which the meat was boiled. Use some of it with milk in making "cream gravy."

RABBIT STEW Mrs. J. G. Sherer

Rub the inside of a saucepan with a dose of garlic; put in pieces of hare left; add three-quarters cup of stewed tomatoes; two raw carrots, cut into small cubes; one small onion, sliced; a teaspoonful of chopped parsley, and about a cup of hot water. Cover tightly and cook until the potatoes are tender (and carrots). Thicken and serve in a border of steamed rice and serve with tiny dumplings.

BELGIAN HARE EN CASSEROLE Mrs. J. G. Sherer

Separate a dressed hare into pieces of desired shape; rub each piece with a little lemon juice and oil which have been stirred together. Let the meat stand covered a few hours; sprinkle with paprika and brown each piece in a little fat in a "sizzling hot" frying pan. Some use two or three slices of fat bacon cut into small pieces for the browning. When golden brown, put the meat in the casserole, cover with boiling water; cover and place in a very moderate oven. At the end of half an hour add two cups of stock or hot water; one tablespoonful of lemon juice, or vinegar, a bit of bay leaf and two teaspoonfuls of onion juice. Cook in a moderate oven about three hours. Bring to the table without removing the cover. And if you have any of the Belgian Hare en Casserole left, make for lunch the next day, the savory little Rabbit Stew.

CHOP SUEY Mrs. J. G. Sherer

One pound veal; one pound pork; one can mushrooms; eight stalks celery; fifteen onions; two tablespoonfuls molasses; little flour on top. Cut meat in small pieces and simmer about twenty minutes; add mushrooms and molasses; then celery and onions. Cook slowly until tender. Sprinkle a little flour over it and mix well; then salt, paprika and about three tablespoonfuls or more (to taste) of chop suey sauce. Simmer meat without water; serve with boiled rice.

CHOP SUEY Mrs. C. S. Junge

Cut tender, fresh, lean pork, chicken, veal or all of these into thin, inch squares and saute well in bacon fat. Have ready one-half as much in bulk of celery; cut in inch pieces and an onion; saute these in same fat. After this, saute mushrooms; put altogether and barely cover with hot water, chicken or veal broth. Add Chinese potatoes and sprouted barley, if they can be procured; add one tablespoonful of molasses; one teaspoonful of salt; one teaspoonful of Chinese Soy; a dash of pepper and put in cooker for three hours or more.

CHOP SUEY Mrs. W. F. Barnard

One pound pork from shoulder; one pound veal from leg; fry one-half hour in a little fat. When brown, add a little water and cook ten minutes, and add one cup celery cut up; one onion, cut up. When nearly done, sprinkle with flour enough to thicken, add two tablespoonfuls of molasses. Serve with rice.

CHESTNUT STUFFING Mrs. S. E. Baumgardner

Shell and blanch four cupfuls French chestnuts; cook in boiling salted water until tender; put through a ricer; season with salt, pepper and a little nutmeg; two tablespoonfuls butter and one-half cupful of cream. Add this to your regular bread mixture for stuffing fowl.

CHESTNUT STUFFING

Shell and blanch French chestnuts, there should be two cups. Cook in boiling salted water until soft. Drain, mash and pass through a potato ricer; add one-four cup butter; one teaspoonful salt; one-eighth teaspoonful pepper; a few grains nutmeg and one-half cup cream. Melt one-fourth cup butter, pour over one cup soft bread crumbs; mix well; combine mixtures and use as filling for turkey, capon or guinea chicken.

OYSTER DRESSING FOR FOWLS Mrs. W. S. Kiskaddon

For an eight or ten-pound turkey cut the brown crust from slices of stale bread until you have as much as the inside of a pound loaf. Put into a suitable dish and pour tepid water over it; take up a handful at the time and squeeze it hard and dry with both hands, placing it as you go along in another dish; now when all is pressed dry, toss it all up lightly through your fingers; now add pepper and salt—about a tablespoonful—also powdered summer savory and sage, and one pint of oysters drained and slightly chopped. For geese and ducks the dressing may be made the same.

RICE DRESSING FOR DUCK OR GOOSE Mrs. H. P. E. Hafer

Boil one cup of rice tender. Chop one stalk celery; two onions; one outside of green pepper; a little piece of garlic; fry in butter and add boiled

SAUCES

HOLLANDAISE SAUCE Mrs. A. Donald Campbell

One tablespoonful flour and one teaspoonful butter; mix over fire until smooth; add, gradually, one pint of boiling water, until all is the consistency of cream. Boil for two or three minutes and season with one salt spoon of salt; one-half teaspoonful mustard; one-quarter teaspoonful pepper. Take from fire and add yolks of two eggs, well beaten; mixing all until smooth. Add slowly, three tablespoonfuls oil and one tablespoonful vinegar. Lemon juice instead of vinegar makes it much more delicate.

HOLLANDAISE SAUCE Belle Shaw

Two tablespoonfuls butter; one tablespoonful flour; one-half pint boiling water; one-half teaspoonful salt; add gradually yolks of two eggs, well beaten; juice of one-half lemon; one-half teaspoonful onion juice; cook over hot water. Be careful not to get sauce too thick.

TARTAR SAUCE NO. 1 Mrs. Carl S. Junge

Sweet cucumber pickles; green peppers and onion. Chop fine and mix with mayonnaise salad dressing.

TARTAR SAUCE NO. 2 Mrs. Carl S. Junge

Tablespoonful mixed capers; tablespoonful cucumber pickles, chopped; teaspoonful parsley; teaspoonful Tarragon; teaspoonful mixed mustard; one-half pint mayonnaise dressing.

RICH GRAVY WITHOUT MEAT Mrs. T. M. Butler

Heat a sufficient amount of lard or drippings in a skillet into which two or three tablespoonfuls of flour have been stirred until a very light brown; then add two-thirds milk to one-third water and season with salt and pepper, adding a level teaspoonful of extract of beef and stir until completely dissolved.

A VEGETABLE SAUCE

One-half teaspoonful kitchen boquet; one level tablespoonful flour; two tablespoonfuls butter; one-fourth teaspoonful salt; two cupfuls hot milk; two egg yolks; blend flour and butter; add salt and milk and boil until smooth and of the desired thickness. Then gradually add the yolks of eggs and kitchen boquet. This may be served on any vegetable desired.

CREOLE SAUCE

One teaspoonful Kitchen Boquet; one onion; five shallots; two green peppers; one tablespoonful butter; one tablespoonful flour; four large tomatoes; one-half bean garlic; one teaspoonful salt; one teaspoonful sugar; six canned mushrooms; one-half teaspoonful parsley. Slice fine onion, shallots and pepper. Cook in butter to a light brown; stir constantly. Then the garlic minced, and the flour. Stir all together and add tomatoes, seasoning, mushrooms, and parsley. Cook twenty minutes, stirring occasionally. Just before serving, add one teaspoonful Kitchen Boquet.

MUSHROOM SAUCE

Three tablespoonfuls Kitchen Boquet; one-third cupful butter; one-third cupful flour; one teaspoonful salt; dash cayenne; one teaspoonful onion juice; two cupfuls milk; one can mushrooms. Melt the butter, add flour and milk gradually, stirring all the while. When cooked, add the salt, cayenne, onion and kitchen boquet. Drain and chop mushrooms; add to sauce and cook three minutes.

TOMATO CELERY SAUCE

Two teaspoonfuls kitchen boquet; one quart tomatoes; one teaspoonful sugar; three pepper-corns; one tablespoonful butter; one head of celery; one onion; one green pepper; one bay leaf; four cloves; salt and pepper; one tablespoonful flour. Place the tomatoes in a saucepan; add the celery cut up into inch lengths; the onion slices and spices. Simmer slowly for twenty minutes, pass through a sieve; return to the fire, and stew down until you have one cupful of puree. Blend the flour and butter together in a double boiler; stir in the tomato-celery puree, and stir until smooth and thick; season with kitchen boquet, salt and pepper. If too thick, add a little water or stock. This is fine to serve with meat loaf, salmon loaf or rice croquettes, etc.

SAUCE BERNAISE

Heat a granite saucepan slightly and break into it four eggs. Beat the eggs briskly over a slow fire, but do not let them boil; mix four tablespoonfuls hot water and two tablespoonfuls beef extract, and as the eggs begin to cook stir in the mixture, adding the juice of one lemon, one tablespoonful onion juice and one teaspoonful Tarragon vinegar, salt and pepper. When this is well mixed pour on beef-steak and serve.

MINT SAUCE

One bunch mint; one tablespoonful sugar; three-fourths cup vinegar. Rinse the mint in cold water; chop very fine; dissolve the sugar in the vinegar; add the mint; let it stand for one hour to infuse before using. If the same is wanted hot, heat the vinegar and stir in the mint just before using.

SAUCE ALLEMANDE Mrs. Bertha C. Hansen

Four tablespoonfuls butter; four tablespoonfuls flour; one egg yolk; one cup white stock; one cup cream; one-half teaspoonful salt; few grains pepper. Make same as a thin white sauce. Just before serving, add the yolk of one egg and cook slightly.

HORSE-RADISH DRESSING FOR ROAST BEEF Mrs. E. D. Gotchy

To a cup of grated horse-radish, add two tablespoonfuls of sugar; one-half teaspoonful salt; one-half cup thick, sweet, cream. Mix the ingredients thoroughly, then add vinegar to taste.

VEGETABLES

"Oh, muckle is the powerful grace
That lies in herbs."

A PORTO RICAN DINNER Mrs. G. W. Plummer

One quart cooked red kidney beans (canned beans are good and save fire); four good sized ripe tomatoes (or the solid tomatoes from a can); four medium sized onions; four green sweet peppers; one-fourth pound nut meats (pecans, almonds or English walnuts are best); two dozen green olives; salt to taste.

Process: If tomatoes are fresh, skin and put in a chopping bowl with onions and peppers, which last should have seeds and white fiber first removed; chop all until about size of a lima bean. Put into skillet a heaping tablespoonful of drippings, from ham or bacon preferred; when hot add chopped vegetables and cook until all are soft and well blended. About fifteen minutes before serving add nut meats and olives cut into strips. In the meantime, heat the beans by themselves; turn all together and cook ten minutes, when it is ready to serve.

Service: Half an hour before time to serve, wash well, enough rice to make a border around your chop platter. Put it into gallopin boiling water, quite heavily salted; water should be at least four times quantity of rice. Boil until barely done; drain in a collander and set to drain in the mouth of the oven for five minutes.

Dispose around the edge of the platter; pour the bean mixture (which should be moist), in the middle, garnish with a wreath of parsley between rice and beans.

This, with a green salad and French dressing is an abundant and satisfying dinner. No meat should be served.

STUFFED POTATOES

Select large uniform sized potatoes. Scrub them with a vegetable brush. Bake in a hot oven, the temperature of the oven should be such that it will bake a potato of medium size in forty to forty-five minutes. Remove a thin slice from the side lengthwise of potatoes; scoop out the pulp, pass through the ricer; add two tablespoonfuls of butter or bacon fat; moisten with hot milk; add two tablespoonfuls each finely chopped chives or onion. Season with salt and pepper, beat thoroughly and return to the shells, using pastry bag and tube, brush over with slightly beaten egg and return to oven to brown delicately.

A "DIFFERENT" DINNER Mrs. G. W. Plummer

A fine, firm head of cauliflower; enough rice to form a border for your chop platter; four tablespoonfuls grated or shredded ripe cheese; one teacupful rich milk; two tablespoonfuls bacon drippings. Garnish with blanched lettuce leaves, canned pimento and parsley.

Process: Wash, trim and put to boil in a large granite or aluminum kettle, the whole head of cauliflower in plenty of salted water. Do not cover. When about half done, put into an iron skillet two tablespoonfuls of bacon drippings and when smoking hot turn in the dry rice which has previously been well washed and dried on a clean towel. Parch this rice in the drippings, stirring constantly until a golden brown. Then dip the water in which the cauliflower boils, spoonful by spoonful, into the rice; as it absorbs the water add more until the rice is puffed, dry and thoroughly done; a little onion may be cooked in with rice if liked. In the meantime make a fine, thick white sauce, using butter and twice the quantity of flour; cook but do not brown; add milk and rub smooth; add shredded cheese, red pepper and salt; cook to a smooth masking sauce.

Service: Put cauliflower, unbroken, in center of platter; mask with sauce and sprinkle with grated cheese. Around the flower dispose the lettuce in such a way as to simulate a growing head. Encircle this with border of rice and put an outside border of parsley. The pimento should be cut in strips and laid up the sides of flower inside lettuce leaves.

SUNDAY NIGHT SUPPER DISH Mrs. G. W. Plummer

Wash round, solid, medium sized tomatoes (one for each service) and cut in half but do not skin. Insert slivers of onion in each half tomato on cut side. Dip cut side in egg, beaten with a little water, seasoned with salt and paprika; then in rolled bread crumbs or rolled shredded wheat biscuit. Two tablespoonfuls of bacon drippings heated to a smoke in skillet or on cake griddle. Put in tomatoes, cut side down, and fry until a golden brown; then turn carefully; reduce heat and cook gently until cooked but not broken. Remove to platter and place on each a generous spoonful of the following sauce:

Sauce: Add dripping to that in skillet in which tomatoes were cooked to make two tablespoonfuls; add four tablespoonfuls flour; one thin slice of onion and cook four minutes; add two cups milk; celery salt, salt and pepper and when incorporated add one-half cupful grated or shredded cheese and cook until smooth.

CUBAN RICE Mrs. W. F. Barnard

One and one-half pounds fresh pork, ground; one onion, chopped; one egg; salt and pepper. Make into little round balls. One quart of tomatoes, strained. Boil meat balls in tomato juice for one hour. Cook rice and serve as a vegetable, pouring meat and tomatoes around it on platter.

INDIAN VEGETABLE CURRY Mrs. Jean Wallace Butler

One pound can baked beans; one pound can lima beans; one pound can green string beans; one pound can wax beans; two pound can tomatoes; eight large onions; one heaping teaspoonful Cross & Blackwell's curry; one tablespoonful salad oil. Remove all vegetables from cans; heat the beans in large cooking vessel; heat tomatoes separately, seasoning very strongly with salt and pepper. Slice onions and boil in water. When sufficiently cooked, add onions and tomatoes to other vegetables. Fry curry in salad oil to a nice brown. Add to the vegtables, and simmer half an hour. While this is simmering, boil rice to serve on plate with curry. This serves ten people. In winter time, for large family you can double recipe, and keep frozen. Better every time reheated. No bread, butter or anything else is served with this, except Indian chutney.

POTATO PUFF BALLS

Scoop out the inside of hot baked potatoes, force the pulp through a ricer, there should be two cups. Add two tablespoonfuls butter; moisten with rich cream; season with salt and paprika, while beating constantly; add one slightly beaten egg yolk and one-half teaspoonful finely chopped parsley; cook one minute, stirring constantly. Remove from range and fold in the stiffly beaten white of one egg. Shape in balls and roll in finely chopped seasoned nut meats; place on buttered pan and brown delicately in the oven. Arrange around broiled whitefish.

POTATO FLUFF Mrs. W. D. Hurlbut

Pass enough hot boiled potatoes through a ricer to make three cups; season with pepper, salt, a big piece of butter and half a cup of cream; beat an egg very light, beat it in the potato; turn into a buttered baking dish; sprinkle bread crumbs on top and bake until browned.

STUFFED SWEET POTATOES Mrs. Louis Geyler

Bake three large sweet potatoes; cut in halves lengthwise; carefully scoop out pulp and press through a ricer. Reserve the shells. Season with one-half teaspoonful of salt; one-fourth teaspoonful paprika; one-half tablespoonful powdered sugar; three tablespoonfuls butter; and one-third cup hot cream or rich milk. Beat them thoroughly, then stir in one-half cup finely chopped almonds, blanched; refill shells. Cut marshmallows in four pieces and cover each portion. Bake in a moderate oven until heated through and marshmallows are delicately browned.

FRENCH FRIED SWEET POTATOES Mrs. A. M. Cameron

Wash and peel very large sweet potatoes and cut lengthwise; as you would white potatoes; fry in the same manner and sprinkle lightly with salt; serve at once.

SWEET POTATO CROQUETTES

Two cupfuls of mashed sweet potatoes; one cupful of hot milk; two eggs; one teaspoonful salt; two tablespoonfuls of butter; bread crumbs; one tablespoonful of butter. Beat the potatoes and milk, gradually stir in the melted butter; salt and one of the eggs well beaten. Form into croquette balls; dip in beaten egg and bread crumbs. Fry in deep fat until golden brown. Drain on paper and serve with cream sauce.

POTATO SURPRISE

Prepare a rich mashed potato in the usual way, using six medium-sized potatoes and hot cream instead of milk. Beat until fluffy, then add one tablespoonful each finely chopped chives or onion juice and one tablespoonful parsley; add one-third cup finely minced ham. Beat again and turn into a buttered baking dish, piling it well in the center. Cover lightly with buttered cracker crumbs, well seasoned with salt and pepper. Bake in oven fifteen minutes. Serve in baking dish.

MASHED POTATOES WITH GREEN PEPPERS AND ONIONS Mrs. W. D. Hurlbut

Pass through a ricer six large hot boiled potatoes; add two tablespoonfuls butter and gradually one-third cupful hot thin cream; season with salt and whip until light and fluffy. Parboil a green pepper (removing seeds and veins) eight minutes; drain and chop fine; mix with two tablespoonfuls finely chopped onion; add gradually to potatoes and heat again. Serve immediately with roast goose, duck or pork.

JUMBALAYA Mrs. M. T. Wagner

One minced onion fried in butter; one-half cup of ham minced; one cup of rice; four cups of tomato juice (if there is not juice enough in a can of tomatoes to make the required quantity, add water); one teaspoonful curry powder; one teaspoonful thyme; a few bay leaves broken up fine; three teaspoonfuls salt and a few grains of cayenne. Mix all together and bake one and one-quarter hours.

SAVORY RICE Mrs. W. R. McGhee

Cook one cupful rice, well washed, in three quarts boiling salted water until partly done; drain; add to rice two cupfuls well seasoned chicken broth; put into double boiler and let it steam until rice is soft and stock is absorbed. Stir in one-fourth cup butter and one tablespoonful finely chopped chives or onion; if onion is used then add one-half tablespoonful chopped parsley.

EASY RICE CROQUETTES Mrs. C. A. Carscadin

Two cups boiled rice (salted); one beaten egg; grated rind of one lemon; add to rice, roll in flour; fry in hot lard. Lay on brown paper and sprinkle well with sugar. Have rice as soft as possible.

STUFFED TOMATOES WITH SHRIMP Mrs. J. E. Kelly

Use six large tomatoes, and scrape out pulp; put little butter in pan and fry the pulp with one small onion, cut fine, and one can of shrimps; add one egg (beaten), and enough bread crumbs to make soft filling. Season with salt and pepper. Fill tomatoes, and sprinkle dry bread crumbs, or cracker crumbs, over top and small piece of butter on each. Bake fifteen minutes and serve hot.

RICE WITH TOMATOES AND GREEN PEPPERS

Finely chop one Bermuda onion, two green peppers; mix with one cup minced raw ham. Saute ten minutes (without browning) in four tablespoonfuls butter. Add one cup of washed rice and three cups of chicken stock or beef broth. Simmer one-half hour stirring occasionally with a fork. Then add four tomatoes peeled and chopped; one-half tablespoonful salt; a few grains cayenne and one-fourth teaspoonful paprika. Cover and cook over hot water until rice is tender. Serve as a vegetable.

SPAGHETTI—ITALIAN STYLE Mrs. J. H. Shanley

One package spaghetti, unbroken, boiled until tender, then let cold water run through it. Fill iron spider with sliced onions and cook until tender, not brown; add two small green peppers, chopped fine; one can mushrooms and one pound chopped steak. Cook together long enough to season, about ten minutes. Put in with the spaghetti in a baking dish, and add one quart tomatoes, strained. Mix thoroughly and sprinkle with grated cheese, viz: layer of spaghetti, then cheese, etc. Also put cheese on top to form crust. Bake until heated through.

ITALIAN SPAGHETTI Mrs. C. A. Jennings

One heaping tablespoonful butter; two medium-sized onions; one bead of garlic; one can tomatoes; two-thirds package spaghetti. Cut onions and garlic fine and put in saucepan to fry with butter a light brown. Add the tomatoes, strained and let simmer one hour. Put spaghetti in large vessel of salted boiling water and keep boiling fast for forty minutes. Have hot dish ready; into this put spaghetti and tomatoes and a small cup of grated Herkimer or other snappy American cheese. Mix thoroughly; serve with small dish of same cheese to springle over spaghetti at table.

SCALLOPED TOMATOES Alice Clock

One No. 3 size tin of tomatoes; one medium-sized onion; six slices bacon; two cups fresh bread crums. Chop the onion and bacon, fry to crisp brown; place first a layer of tomatoes, then a layer of bread crumbs, then a layer of onion and bacon; over which salt and pepper is shaken. Repeat layers until all material is used. Bake forty-five minutes in moderate oven.

ITALIAN MACARONI Mrs. W. I. Clock

One-half pound streaky salt pork, no bones, very little lean meat; three onions; a suspicion of garlic; one teacup of chopped parsley; one No. 3 can of tomatoes; four heaping teaspoonfuls granulated sugar; one teaspoonful salt; one-fourth teaspoonful pepper; two tablespoonfuls of grated Parmesan cheese; one pound of spaghetti. Put finely chopped pork, onions and parsley into frying pan and fry to nice brown; add sugar, salt, pepper and cheese. At same time the above is cooking have the tomatoes heating in enameled saucepan; also have water boiling ready to put spaghetti in, for it must actually boil twenty-five minutes to be tender. After the tomatoes have cooked about ten minutes, put through sieve and add to pork and onions and let all simmer while spaghetti cooks. Put spaghetti in collander to drain. Serve by placing a layer of spaghetti in deep dish, then sauce and cheese, and so on each layer until all material is used; serve very hot.

MACARONI Mrs. Gussie Enos

Boil macaroni one-half hour. Put one pint milk; one and one-half cups grated cheese; one tablespoonful butter; one tablespoonful flour; salt and pepper together and boil all until smooth. Put layer of macaroni and layer of sauce with sauce on top. Bake one-half hour.

HOMINY CROQUETTES

To one-half cup hominy (taken from a carton); add two cups hot stewed and strained tomato pulp; cook in a double boiler until hominy is tender. Stir in two tablespoonfuls butter; three-fourths teaspoonful salt; one-fourth teaspoonful paprika. Spread mixture on a plate to cool. Then shape into balls the size of small lemons, roll in crumbs, dip in egg and again in crumbs and fry in hot deep fat. Drain on brown paper and serve with cheese sauce.

HOMINY GRITS Mrs. W. D. Hurlbut

Put two cupfuls of milk and two of water into a double boiler; add a little salt and one cupful of hominy grits; let boil hard one hour; do not stir. The moisture will all be absorbed and it will be light and creamy. Use as a vegetable or in place of potatoes.

TOMATOES, CREOLE STYLE

Wash and wipe the desired number of medium-sized tomatoes. Cut a slice from the blossom ends, scoop out pulp, sprinkle with salt in the inside, invert on plate, let stand one hour. Melt two tablespoonfuls butter, add two tablespoonfuls flour mixed with one-half teaspoonful salt, one-fourth teaspoonful paprika and few grains cayenne. Stir until blended, then pour on slowly one-half cup cream. Stir until smooth and add one cup green corn, cut from cob, and mixed with one-half tablespoonful each red and green pepper, finely chopped. Flavor delicately with onion juice. Fill tomatoes, cover with buttered crumbs and bake in moderate oven until tomatoes and corn are tender.

TOMATOES ON HALF SHELL Mrs. R. McNeil

Cut tomatoes in half without peeling. Place them in baking dish. Put in a piece of butter on each, and dust with salt and pepper. Put in oven and cook until tender. Have ready squares of toasted bread. On each place a half tomato and pour around white sauce and serve hot.

BAKED TOMATOES Mrs. W. O. King

Select nice smooth tomatoes; slice off top and remove pulp and seeds. Rub this through collander. Add one-half cup of each bread and cracker crumbs, pepper, salt and minced onion to tomatoes with a little butter. Stuff tomatoes, place top on, using toothpicks; bake one hour in a moderate oven.

FRIED TOMATOES Mrs. C. S. Junge

Green or ripe tomatoes may be used. Slice and dip in flour. Place in skillet with plenty of bacon fat and a little butter. Fry until brown and lift carefully onto a platter. In the remaining fat stir a tablespoonful of flour, then pour a cup and a half of milk. When creamed, turn over tomatoes and serve.

BAKED NOODLES Mrs. E. Lewis Phelps

One box of home made noodles, boil until tender then drain. Butter a baking dish; put in a layer of noodles; sprinkle with grated cheese and seasoning; then another layer of noodles; then two cups of cooked boiled ham chopped fine; chopped green pepper and chopped onion; put the remainder of noodles on top and add cheese, etc. Beat up four or five eggs; add milk enough to cover all the noodles. Set pan into pan of water and bake slowly until eggs are done. Can add buttered cracker crumbs on top if liked.

CORN PUDDING Helen M. Bailey

Six ears corn; two eggs; one-half pint milk; pinch salt; pinch pepper; cut corn from cob, beat eggs, and add milk, eggs and seasoning to corn. Bake until light brown.

CORN OYSTERS Mrs. E. S. Smith

Mix one pint of grated corn; three tablespoonfuls of milk; one teacup of flour; a piece of butter the size of an egg. Drop by dessertspoonfuls into a little hot butter. Fry on both sides.

CORN CROQUETTES

One cupful of stewed or canned corn; one-half cupful of dried bread crumbs; one-half cupful of milk; one beaten egg; one teaspoonful of salt; one teaspoonful of baking powder; one tablespoonful of flour. Chop corn, mix with bread crumbs, milk and other ingredients. Drop from spoon into deep fat and fry until light brown.

GREEN PEPPERS STUFFED WITH RICE, TOMATOES AND NUT MEATS

Cut a slice from the stem ends of six medium-sized mild, green peppers; remove seeds and veins; parboil in boiling water eight minutes. Drain. Have ready one and one-half cups hot boiled rice; mix with three-fourths cup thick tomato puree; add one cup chopped English walnut meats. Season with salt, pepper and a few grains of cayenne; add one teaspoonful each finely chopped parsley and chives or onion. Fill peppers. Arrange on buttered dripping pan; cover with buttered cracker crumbs and bake in oven until heated through and crumbs are brown.

GREEN PEPPERS STUFFED WITH CORN Mrs. T. D. Caliger

Select sweet green peppers of medium size; cut a thick slice from stem ends; remove seeds and veins. Soak in salt water one hour, drain, and fill with following mixture. Put three cups of canned corn into a saucepan, with two tablespoonfuls finely chopped green peppers, butter and one tablespoonful of onion juice. Simmer slowly fifteen minutes, stirring often to prevent burning. Cover tops of peppers with buttered bread crumbs, and bake one-half hour in moderate oven.

EGG PLANT AND SHRIMP Mrs. Ada Woods

Boil a whole egg plant, cutting off the stem end. When done take off skin and put the inside to drain. Put a cup of stale bread crumbs, a grated onion, salt and pepper, tablespoonful parsley and a clove of garlic minced fine, in a skillet with two tablespoonfuls bacon drippings, and fry until brown; add this to the egg plant, put in two dozen shrimps, broken up, and when all is well mixed put in the oven and brown.

FRENCH FRIED EGG PLANT Mrs. A. M. Cameron

Prepare egg plant in the usual way; drain and cut as you would potatoes for French fry; sprinkle with salt, pepper and flour; place in a frying basket and fry strips until crisp and a pretty brown; drain on brown paper.

BAKED STUFFED EGG PLANT

Cut slice from stem end; reserve for cover, scoop out inside, leaving a wall one-fourth inch thick, sprinkle inside with salt and pepper, finely chop pulp. Cook one-half onion, finely chopped, in one tablespoonful butter three minutes without browning, add three fresh mushrooms, finely chopped, four tablespoonfuls finely chopped lean raw ham, season with salt, pepper; cook five minutes, stirring constantly. Add egg plant pulp, three-fourths cup soft bread crumbs, one-half teaspoonful finely chopped parsley. Mix well, refill shell, cover with buttered crumbs. Bake in moderate oven forty-five minutes.

NEW STRING BEANS Mrs. W. D. Hurlbut

Cut two thin slices of bacon crosswise in narrow shreds, using shears for this purpose. Saute to a delicate brown. Add two cups hot, cooked, well-drained string beans and one-half tablespoonful grated onion or onion juice. Shake the frying pan to thoroughly mix the ingredients, season with salt and pepper. Turn into hot serving dish.

CREAMED PEAS AS AN ENTREE Mrs. C. A. Carscadin

Cut with a cookie cutter a round of bread from a thick slice, then a ring with a doughnut cutter. Dip in melted butter and toast a delicate brown in the oven. Fill them with peas in cream sauce.

FRENCH FRIED ONIONS Bertha Z. Bishee

Peel onions, slice and separate rings. Beat an egg, white and yolk together; salt and pepper to taste and stir in enough flour—about a tablespoonful—to make a thin batter. Pour over the onion rings, making sure that they are well coated, and fry a handful at a time in deep fat, which must be hot enough to brown quickly. Drain and serve covered with a napkin.

BAKED SPANISH ONION Alice Clock

Three Spanish onions; two cups of fresh bread crumbs; one pint milk; one heaping tablespoonful butter. Take greased baking dish. Place alternate layers of sliced onion, and bread crumbs, seasoning each layer with salt and pepper. When materials are used up, pour over the pint of milk; and the butter cut in small pieces is placed on the top last. Bake slowly, until onion can be pierced easily.

SCALLOPED CABBAGE Miss Kennedy

Cut one-half of boiled cabbage in small pieces; sprinkle with salt, pepper and one finely chopped pimento; pour over one and one-fourth cups thin white sauce, mixed with one-third cup grated cheese. Mix well and turn into a buttered baking dish; cover with buttered and seasoned cracker crumbs. Place in oven and bake until crumbs are brown.

CABBAGE ROLLS Mrs. C. S. Junge

Parboil in salt water the large leaves of a cabbage. Take them from the water and place singly on the cake board and pepper them. Mix half and half, chopped beef and pork and season. Make into rolls twice the size of an egg. Round these roll several cabbage leaves and fasten with tooth picks. Place these in the skillet with two tablespoonfuls of bacon fat or lard with a little butter. Turn in a small amount of water and cook covered over a slow fire. When water cooks off add more in small quantities for nearly an hour. Remove tooth picks and serve.

CAULIFLOWER AU GRATIN Miss June Baumgardner

Boil cauliflower until tender; separate so that a flower will be in each ramekin. Make a white sauce and grate three tablespoonfuls yellow American cheese in it; when the cheese is melted pour over the vegetable in ramekin, put a few buttered bread crumbs on top and put in the oven to brown.

PARSNIP SAUTE

Wash parsnips and cook until tender in boiling water. Drain and cover with cold water; with the hands slip off the skins. Mash and rub through a strainer. Season pulp with salt, pepper and butter, shape in flat cakes and dredge with flour. Saute a golden brown in equal parts hot butter and chicken fat.

FRIED SUMMER SQUASH

Wash, wipe and cut tender squash in one-half inch slices, sprinkle with salt, pepper and dredge with flour, dip in egg, then in fine cracker crumbs, repeat and fry in deep, hot fat, drain and serve.

CREAMED CELERY CABBAGE Mrs. H. Clay Calhoun

Cut celery cabbage in inch lengths, boil until tender in salted water; drain and pour over a rich cream sauce.

BAKED, STUFFED ARTICHOKES Mrs. Francis A. Sieber

Six artichokes; four ounces fat pork; two cups chopped mushrooms; two tablespoonfuls chopped shallots; one teaspoonful minced parsley; one tablespoonful flour; one tablespoonful butter; one-half cup spinach sauce; one-half teaspoonful salt, a little pepper, nutmeg; one cup broth; one glass white wine. Prepare artichokes, boil thirty minutes and drain. Mince pork and fry with shallots; add mushrooms and parsley and simmer ten minutes. Blend with it the flour mixed with butter; add Spanish sauce and seasoning. Stuff artichokes, and tie each with string; brown outside in a little olive oil, add the broth and wine. Cover and cook forty minutes in moderate oven. When they are ready to serve remove the strings and arrange on a hot platter and pour the sauce over them. Garnish with a whole mushroom on top of each.

MUSHROOMS Mrs. H. P. E. Hafer

Peal one pound fresh mushrooms. Fry in butter slowly for three-quarters of an hour. Add two cups of soup stock and one-half cup of cream and thicken with flour. Serve on toast.

STUFFED MUSHROOMS Mrs. K. Larson

Brush twelve large mushrooms. Remove stems. Chop finely, and peel caps. Melt three tablespoonfuls butter, and one-half tablespoonful finely chopped shallot, and chopped stems. Then cook ten minutes. Add one and one-half tablespoonfuls of flour, chicken stock to moisten, a slight grating of nutmeg, and one-half teaspoonful finely chopped parsley, salt and pepper to taste. Cool mixture and fill caps, well rounding over top. Cover with buttered cracker crumbs, and bake fifteen minutes in a hot oven.

STEWED MUSHROOMS Mrs. E. R. Hornig

Peel and wash mushrooms, cut one or two onions very fine and stew in a tablespoonful of butter, add mushrooms, season with pepper and salt and sprinkle over a little flour. Cook about fifteen minutes and serve hot.

STEWED CUCUMBERS Mrs. E. R. Hornig

Pare and cut lengthwise in quarters, remove seeds. Put into hot butter, or finely cut bacon, season with salt and pepper. Cook about fifteen minutes over a slow fire, or until they appear glossy. Add a teaspoonful vinegar or a little sour cream. Serve hot.

FRIED CUCUMBERS Mrs. William H. Fahrney

Peel and slice, medium thick, large cucumbers; dip in batter and cracker crumbs and fry in hot fat until brown.

KOHLRABBI Mrs. E. R. Hornig

Take three bunches of kohlrabbi, remove hard leaves, strip tender leaves from their ribs, cut them up fine. Peel kohlrabbi, cut in slices quarter of an inch thick, and add tender green leaves. Put on to boil with cold water, just enough to cover, until tender. Season with pepper and salt, blend a teaspoonful of flour with butter, add to vegetable, and stew a few minutes longer. Serve hot.

SALADS

"'Twould tempt the dying anchorite to eat;
Back to the world, he'd turn his weary soul,
And plunge his fingers in the salad bowl."

TEA SALAD Mrs. Frederick Dunn

Upon a leaf of head lettuce, place a round of boiled ham. (One slice of ham will make two rounds.) Then place a thick slice of tomato; and next a half a hard boiled egg, cut crosswise; then a ring of sweet green peppers; and over all pour Thousand Island dressing. Garnish with parsley and radish rosettes. Two such portions served on a salad plate makes an appetizing dish, or it can be served on a large platter at the table, or passed.

PERFECTION SALAD Mrs. Louis Geyler

One envelope Knox's sparkling gelatine; one-half cup cold water; one-half cup mild vinegar; one pint boiling water; one teaspoonful salt; one cup finely shredded celery; one cucumber chopped finely; one bunch radishes chopped; one green pepper chopped; one-half cup sugar; juice of one lemon; little onion juice; seeds of one pomegranite. Soak gelatine in cold water five minutes; add vinegar; lemon juice; onion juice; boiling water; sugar and salt. Strain and when beginning to set, add ingredients. Turn into ring mold and chill. Serve on lettuce leaves, garnish with asparagus tips in center and tomatoes quartered around it. Use cooked mayonnaise as dressing.

CHICKEN SALAD Mrs. Jarvis Weed

To the white meat and a very little bit of the dark meat of a chicken add one cupful blanched almonds, a cupful of celery and about six slices of Hawaiian pineapple shredded. Cover with an oil mayonnaise and mix well.

FROZEN FRUIT SALAD Mrs. C. H. Bushnell

Three cakes blue label cream cheese; one-half pint mayonnaise dressing; one pint whipped cream; one ten-cent bottle maraschino cherries; one can white cherries; one can pineapple cut fine; one-half cup pecan nuts. Beat cheese to cream, mix with fruit, put in melon mold and freeze about three hours. Serve on lettuce with mayonnaise.

FROZEN SALAD Mrs. A. E. Kaltenbrun

Five eggs beaten separately. One cup of vinegar; one cup of milk and cream mixed; one tablespoonful butter; one-half teaspoonful mustard; one-fourth teaspoonful salt; one cup of sugar. Cook until thick. Let cool and add: two bottles whipping cream, any kind of fruit—preferably pineapple, oranges, peaches, etc., and freeze like a mousse. Baking powder can molds are splendid. Slice and serve with cherry on lettuce.

FROZEN SALAD Mrs. Thos. D. Caliger

Melt one tablespoonful butter and add yolks of two eggs, well beaten; mix three and one-half tablespoonfuls flour, three tablespoonfuls sugar, one teaspoonful salt, one-third teaspoonful paprika, few grains cayenne. Add to the above mixture: Two-thirds cup milk; one-third cup vinegar. Cook same in double boiler until thick. Stir constantly; when cooked, beat two minutes and chill; then add two large tablespoonfuls of pineapple juice, four cupfuls of fruit cut fine, one bottle of whipped cream. Pack in ice and salt for three hours. Slice and serve on lettuce leaves.

HAWAIIAN SALAD Mrs. C. A. Jennings

One large or two small heads of lettuce; four medium sized tomatoes; one alligator pear. Place lettuce leaves on plate with two or three slices of tomatoes. Cover with rings of alligator pear cut very thin. Serve with French dressing.

French Dressing: Rub salad dish with bead of garlic (omit if objectionable). One-half teaspoonful salt, generous dash of paprika, four tablespoonfuls olive oil, one and one-half tablespoonfuls vinegar. This will serve six people.

COTTAGE CHEESE AND PRUNE SALAD Mrs. Lyman Holsey

One and one-fourth cups cottage cheese; one and one-half dozen medium sized prunes: one-fourth cup chopped hickory nuts; one-fourth teaspoonful salt; dash paprika. Wash prunes. Remove pits and let soak over night. Mix remaining ingredients and stuff prunes with this mixture. Place on lettuce leaf and serve with French dressing.

FRUIT SALAD Belle Hallen Molt

One can pineapple cubed; one pound Malaga grapes seeded and cut in half; one-fourth pound pecans; one-fourth pound marshmallows cut in half.

Dressing: Yolks of four eggs; one-half teaspoonful mustard; one-half teaspoonful salt; juice of one lemon; one-half cup of cream; boil in double boiler until thick and smooth. Let this get cold and add one-half pint whipped cream and pour over and mix thoroughly with fruit and let stand in icebox four hours before serving, giving the marshmallows a chance to become creamy. It will come out like a thick fluff.

FRUIT SALAD Mrs. C. B. Martin

Into a quart of boiling water, put two packages of lemon jello; when thoroughly dissolved, strain; and when cool mix in one cup of chopped nuts; one cup of green grapes, seeded and cut in half; one cup of sliced pineapple; one-half cup pimento; two cups chopped cabbage; stir and add to jello.

FRUIT SALAD Mrs. J. Blackburn

Green California grapes cut in half and seeded, a little celery cut in dice, pecan nuts cut in halves and a few quartered olives. Mix carefully with salad dressing and before serving add one-half cup of cream.

BEST EVER SALAD Mrs. Kathryn M. Haskell

One orange cut in quarters; one banana cut in small oblong pieces; one small can of pineapple cut in small pieces; one-half cup chopped English walnuts.

Dressing: Two eggs beaten lightly; one-fourth cup pineapple juice; one-fourth cup lemon juice; one-half cup sugar; cook until it thickens; let get cold and pour over fruit.

TOMATO STUFFED WITH COTTAGE CHEESE AND ALMONDS
Katherine Blade

Peel nice ripe tomatoes; scoop out the centers and fill with cottage cheese and minced almonds; place a spoonful mayonnaise on top and sprinkle minced almonds over the mayonnaise.

TOMATO EN SURPRISE Mrs. J. E. Kelly

Peel a nice large tomato and empty its contents; take some cold slaw and celery hashed up very fine and mix it with mayonnaise dressing; and add a pinch of salt and a dash of paprika. Mix well and fill the tomato with this mixture. The tomatoes must be served very cold.

A NOVEL SALAD DISH Mrs. Campbell

Take large and long cucumbers, cut them through the middle lengthwise, scrape out the inside and one has a pretty green boat in which to serve the salad. This is particularly pretty with lobster or shrimp salad on account of the contrast in the color.

CHRISTMAS SALAD Marian Blade

Two large grapefruit; one cup chopped celery; one cup chopped tart apples; one-half cup hickory nut meats. Cut grapefruit in small pieces, being careful to remove all partitions and tough parts. Drain off juice, add celery, apples, nuts and mayonnaise. Toss together and serve on small leaves of cabbage. Garnish with round pieces of pimentos to resemble holly berries and pieces of green pepper cut to resemble holly leaves.

DATE AND PINEAPPLE SALAD Mrs. Lyman

One pound dates; four slices pineapple; one cup nut meats. Wash the dates and steam for five minutes, dry in oven. Cut in half removing the seed. Chop nut meats. Cut pineapple into small cubes and mix with nut meats. Marinate with French dressing and stuff dates with mixture. Serve on lettuce leaf with Mayonnaise dressing.

NEAPOLITAN SALAD Mrs. Lyman Holsey

Two cups of cottage cheese; one-half cum cream; one-half teaspoonful salt. Mix cheese with cream and salt. Color one-third of mixture with beet juice, pink. Mold in brick shaped tin which has been dipped in very cold water. Put in a layer of white, then the pink, then white. Chill thoroughly before turning out. Slice with very sharp knife dipped in hot water. Serve on lettuce leaves.

ANCHOVIE BONNES-BOUCHES Mrs. Trumen

Fillet some anchovies, cut them into thin strips, and put them on a dish with some shredded lettuce leaves, small radishes, some capers, thin slices of lemon and chopped parsley. Arrange all tastefully, season with lemon juice mixed with salad oil, garnish with stoned olives and the yolks and the whites of hard boiled eggs.

CUCUMBER SALAD Mrs. J. T. Brown

One cucumber cut very fine; one can grated pineapple; juice of four lemons; sugar to taste; two tablespoonfuls of gelatine. Cook the gelatine in a little water; then add the juice of pineapple and lemons; when it begins to set add the cucumber and pineapple. Put in molds, serve with a cream mayonnaise dressing.

CUCUMBER SALAD Mrs. Maxwell

Peel the cucumbers, cut them in thin slices without cutting the slices off, thus giving the appearance of a whole cucumber. Insert in each opening thin slices of radishes with the peel on, sliced to the exact size of the cucumber. Chill thoroughly and serve with French dressing.

BUTTER BEAN SALAD Mrs. Lyman

One pint butter beans (canned or cooked); one cup chopped celery; one tablespoonful finely chopped onion; one tablespoonfud finely chopped green pepper. Mix ingredients together lightly. Garnish with grated cheese, and serve with French dressing.

CREAM CHEESE Mrs. C. E. Ellis

One Neufachatel cheese; one-half that quantity of butter; one tablespoonful cream; dash of tabasco sauce or cayenne pepper. Tint pink with vegetable coloring; roll in nuts, finely chopped. Serve on a lettuce leaf.

BANANA SALAD

Cut bananas lengthwise, roll them in mayonnaise then in ground peanuts and serve on lettuce leaves.

NORMANDY SALAD Mrs. Theresa B. Orr

One can French peas washed and strained. One-half pound English walnuts cut the size of the peas. Mix dressing with nuts. Toss with peas and serve on lettuce leaves.

PIQUANT RAISINS FOR SALADS Mrs. Lyman

Carefully seed one-half pound cluster raisins. Rinse quickly in hot water and drain well. Add one-fourth cup cold water, let stand one or two hours, then simmer, covered, until raisins begin to plump. Add one tablespoonful of Tarragon vinegar and simmer until vinegar is absorbed. Remove from fire, place tea towel under cover to absorb moisture and let stand until cold. These raisins are used as garnish or component part of salads.

CABBAGE SLAW Mrs. T. M. Butler

Chop up very fine one-half of medium sized cabbage head, one stalk of celery and one sweet pepper, salt to season, add one-half cup of sugar and enough vinegar to moisten the mixture.

POTATO SALAD

Four cupfuls sliced boiled potatoes; one small onion, chopped; one-half cupful weak vinegar; one teaspoonful salt; one-eighth teaspoonful pepper; three tablespoonfuls olive oil; two slices bacon diced; four stalks celery; chopped lettuce; one tablespoonful minced parsley. Put onion in a large bowl, add salt and vinegar, and let stand ten minutes; then slice in the potatoes while still warm and mix thoroughly. Add oil, the celery cut fine, the bacon fried to a crisp, and the bacon fat; then the parsley. Arrange on a bed of lettuce and garnish with beets and hard cooked eggs that have been chopped.

POTATO SALAD Mrs. Campbell

Cut cold boiled potatoes into dice and mix them with two minced raw onions and one tablespoonful minced parsley. Sprinkle with salt and pepper to taste, stir lightly together and add one small diced cucumber and a hard boiled egg, also diced. Set in ice box for an hour. When ready to serve, stir in one cucumber cut into dice and mix with two-thirds cupful of salad dressing. Garnish with hard boiled eggs and olives.

TO SERVE WITH A SALAD Mrs. C. A. Carscadin

Cream together one cake Blue Label Cream Cheese, and one-quarter pound or less of Roquefort cheese; fold into this one bottle of cream whipped stiff. This will serve eight people.

HAM SALAD Edna Blade

Chop one cupful of cooked ham very fine. Soak one tablespoonful of Knox gelatine in one tablespoonful of cold water for half an hour, then dissolve in one cupful of hot water with one teaspoonful each of onion juice and chopped parsley. Add to the ham and stir occasionally until the mixture thickens; fold in one cupful of whipped cream and add one-half saltspoonful of paprika. Form it into little basket shapped molds and, when set, partly fill each little pink basket with mayonnaise. Surround with tiny lettuce leaves and simulate handles by two arched plumes of parsley. Placed on pretty plates, these form a delectable decorative fancy. If the larder does not contain the leftover meat, a can of deviled ham may be substituted.

LOBSTER SALAD Mrs. Campbell

Take a can of lobster, taking care to free it from any pieces of shell; set it on ice while you make a good mayonnaise dressing and set that on ice also. Have ready one-half as much celery as you have lobster, cut into one-half inch lengths; mix lobster meat and celery together, sprinkle with salt and cayenne, then stir in one cup of mayonnaise. Arrange two or three lettuce leaves together to form a shell and put two or three teaspoonfuls of the salad on each. Garnish with hard boiled eggs cut lengthwise.

OYSTER SALAD Miss Anna Brennan

Allow six oysters to each person. Parboil them in their liquid and drain at once. When cool cut each one in four pieces. Break tender young leaves of lettuce and mix in equal parts with oysters. Pour over all the following dressing. Allow one egg to two persons. Boil eggs twenty minutes. When cold cut whites in slices and mix with oysters and lettuce. Mash yolks fine in deep bowl and add one raw yolk. Stir in olive oil slowly until it is a smooth paste. Season with lemon juice, English mustard and salt. Add oil until as thick as cream. Pour over salad.

DANDELION SALAD Mrs. Maxwell

Pick the young tender leaves of the dandelion, wash and lay in ice water for half an hour. Drain, shake dry and pat still drier between the folds of a napkin. Turn into a chilled bowl, cover with a French dressing, turn the greens over and over in this and send at once to the table.

TOMATO JELLY Mrs. A. Donald Campbell

Cook, for twenty minutes, two cups of tomatoes, with slice of onion; one teaspoonful salt; dash of pepper; strain and add one tablespoonful Knox gelatine, which has already been soaked in cold water. Stir all until gelatine is entirely dissolved; then pour in a ring mold that has been dipped in cold water. When ready to serve turn out on a bed of lettuce leaves and fill center with chopped celery well mixed with mayonnaise.

SALAD DRESSING Mrs. H. P. Sieh

One-half cup olive oil; one teaspoonful paprika; one teaspoonful Worcestershire sauce; a pinch mustard; one-half cup sugar; one-third teaspoonful salt. Mix all together well and add vinegar until the right consistency.

SALAD DRESSING Mrs. E. Hilliard

Three yolks of eggs, one tablespoonful sugar, one-quarter teaspoonful mustard; one-tenth teaspoonful cayenne pepper, one tablespoonful salt, one pint sweet oil, few drops at a time, one-quarter cup vinegar, one-quarter cup lemon juice. Add sweet cream before using.

EXCELLENT SALAD DRESSING Mrs. Frederick Dunn

Two tablespoonfuls granulated sugar; two teaspoonfuls dry mustard; little red pepper; eight yolks eggs; eight tablespoonfuls vinegar; two teaspoonfuls salt; two teaspoonfuls butter. Cook in double boiler five minutes; when cold add one cup chopped pecan nuts or blanched almonds, twenty-four chopped marshmallows, two cups whipped cream. Pour over apricots or fruit salad. Garnish with maraschino cherries. This serves sixteen persons.

CREAM SALAD DRESSING Mrs. N. A. Flanders

Two tablespoonfuls butter; two tablespoonfuls sugar; two eggs; one-half cup whipped cream; one-half teaspoonful salt; one-half teaspoonful mustard (together); one-eighth cayenne pepper; one-fourth cup vinegar. Mix sugar, salt and mustard together in small pot, add vinegar and put on fire to heat. Beat eggs very light in a round bottomed bowl. Add the vinegar and other ingredients. Stand bowl in a pan of hot water over fire, and beat with a dover beater until it thickens. Take the bowl out at once and beat in the butter. Set aside to cool. Add whipped cream before serving. (Last item not necessary.)

CREAM SALAD DRESSING Mrs. J. H. Shanley

Four tablespoonfuls butter; one tablespoonful sugar; one-half cupful vinegar; one tablespoonful flour; one teaspoonful each, salt and dry mustard; one cupful milk; three eggs; dash cayenne pepper. Let the butter get hot; add flour and stir until smooth, being careful not to brown. Add milk, stir, and let boil up. Place saucepan in another of hot water; beat eggs, salt, mustard, add vinegar and stir into boiling mixture. Continue stirring until it thickens. When cold, bottle.

MRS. LUFF'S MAYONNAISE

Yolks of three eggs; two teaspoonfuls mustard; one teaspoonful salt; one saltspoonful white pepper; two tablespoonfuls salad oil: two tablespoonfuls sugar; one tablespoonful flour, heaping; one-half cup hot vinegar; one cup milk or cream. Beaten whites added last. Put in double boiler and stir until it begins to thicken. Take it off stove and beat until cool.

FRUIT SALAD DRESSING Mrs. A. R. Swickheimar

Butter size of an egg; three eggs; juice of two oranges; juice of one lemon; one-half can pineapple juice; one-half cup sugar; one-third spoonful dry mustard; one teaspoonful flour. Cook in double boiler until thick; set aside to cool; add one cup of cream, whipped.

FRUIT SALAD DRESSING Mrs. Frank Sessions

Yolks of two eggs, well beaten; two tablespoonfuls each of oil, vinegar and sugar; one-half teaspoonful salt and dash of paprika. Put in bowl over the teakettle, beat until cool. Just before serving add the beaten whites and a little cream.

FRUIT DRESSING Mrs. A. E. Kaltenbrun

To the juice of one can of pineapple add: one tablespoonful flour; one-half cup sugar; a pinch of salt; tablespoonful butter. Cook until creamy, let cool and add one bottle of whipped cream, one-half pound of dates and marshmallows. Serve on fruit.

FRUIT SALAD DRESSING Mrs. T. M. Butler

Two eggs, well beaten, add one cup of sugar; one-half cup of pineapple juice, one-fourth cup of lemon juice or juice of one lemon. Place in double boiler and cook until creamy and thick. Let it cool and just before serving whip one-half pint of cream and stir in the sauce.

SALAD DRESSING Mrs. W. H. Muschlet

One heaping teaspoonful flour; one heaping teaspoonful Colemans mustard; one-half cup granulated sugar; one teaspoonful salt; mix all together. Yolks of three eggs; one-half cup vinegar; one cup cream or cream and milk; large lump butter; little paprika. Cook in double boiler until thickened. Before getting cold stir in the beaten whites.

ITALIAN SALAD DRESSING Mrs. Theresa B. Orr

Yolks of three eggs boiled hard and mashed fine. One small spoonful salt; one small spoonful mustard; a little cayenne pepper; one saltspoonful of powdered sugar; four tablespoonfuls olive oil; one tablespoonful lemon juice; one tablespoonful vinegar. Do not let come to boil but stir constantly.

SOUR CREAM SALAD DRESSING Mrs. A. R. Swickheimar

Three eggs beaten with one cup sour cream; two tablespoonfuls sugar; one-half teaspoonful mustard; one-half cup vinegar; one tablespoonful flour. Cook in double boiler; when cold, add one-third cup olive oil.

THOUSAND ISLAND DRESSING Mrs. Carolyn Chandler

To a foundation of either boiled dressing or mayonnaise, add: Chili sauce, catsup, hard boiled egg and green olives. Serve on either lettuce hearts or French endive.

THOUSAND ISLAND DRESSING Mrs. F. B. Woodland

Three tablespoonfuls mayonnaise dressing; one tablespoonful Tarragon vinegar; two tablespoonfuls chili sauce; one tablespoonful cream; a little dash salt, pepper and paprika; dash English mustard; and some chopped chives or onions.

MRS. PHELPS' THOUSAND ISLAND SALAD DRESSING Mrs. E. Lewis Phelps

Rub the bowl with garlic; two tablespoonfuls cooked salad dressing, cream this with one tablespoonful chives, cut fine; one tablespoonful green pepper and one of red peppers, both cut fine; one tablespoonful roquefort cheese; four tablespoonfuls home made chili sauce.

COOKED SALAD DRESSING Mrs. H. D. Sheldon

One-half tablespoonful salt; one-half tablespoonful flour; two tablespoonfuls sugar; one teaspoonful dry mustard, little cayenne pepper; yolks of two eggs; three-fourths cup milk; one-fourth cup vinegar; butter size of egg. Mix all dry materials, then add eggs well beaten; butter, milk and vinegar. Cook until thick, stirring constantly. Thin with cream.

BOILED DRESSING Mrs. Arthur Hammer

One teaspoonful each of mustard and sugar; two teaspoonfuls flour; one-half teaspoonful salt; one-eighth teaspoonful paprika; one egg and one cup of milk. Have butter the size of an egg hot in a spider; have the above ingredients thoroughly mixed and put in the hot butter, stirring constantly until thick. Add vinegar and lemon to taste and beat until smooth.

WALTHAM SALAD DRESSING B. C. Hansen

One cup of sour cream; two egg yolks; one-fourth cup vinegar; two teaspoonfuls salt; two teaspoonfuls sugar; one teaspoonful mustard; one-eighth teaspoonful pepper. To cream, add egg yolks, slightly beaten, vinegar and remaining ingredients, thoroughly mixed. Cook in double boiler, stirring constantly, until mixture thickens.

ROQUEFORT CHEESE DRESSING Mrs. A. E. Kaltenbrun

Take a ripe piece of cheese, cream with a fork and add cream or vinegar until it makes a paste. Add oil and vinegar, salt and paprika as for French dressing.

CHEESE MAYONNAISE

Half a cream cheese; four tablespoonfuls of olive oil; one tablespoonful of vinegar; one teaspoonful of salt; dash of cayenne. Rub the cheese to a paste with the olive oil, seasonings and vinegar until it is thick like an egg mayonnaise. To some the flavor of oil is unpleasant, but a very good mayonnaise can be made without oil, provided you use two eggs instead of the one egg yolk ordinarily required.

PIES

*"No soil upon earth is so dear to our eyes
As the soil we first stirred in terrestrial
pies."*

PIE CRUST UNFAILING Mrs. H. S. Mount

One cup flour; two tablespoonfuls of lard; three tablespoonfuls of boiling water; pinch salt; baking powder enough to cover the end of silver knife. Put lard into water. Beat well; then add to dry ingredients, and roll out.

PIE CRUST Anna May Price

One cup shortening; one-half cup boiling water; cream. Two cups sifted flour and two level teaspoonfuls baking powder.

PIE CRUST Mrs. N. L. Hurlbut

One cup flour; two heaping tablespoonfuls lard; pinch salt; one teaspoonful baking powder. Cold water enough to make dough. Handle as little as possible.

LEMON CREAM PIE Mrs. Becker

Bake crust separate. One heaping tablespoonful lard; one-half cup flour; two tablespoonfuls water; one-fourth teaspoonful salt. Filling: Two cups water; juice of one lemon; yolks of two eggs; two tablespoonfuls corn starch; one-half cup sugar; pinch of salt. Boil filling separate and when cool fill in baked crust. Beat whites of eggs with two tablespoonfuls sugar and put on the top.

LEMON PIE

Juice of three lemons; three eggs; pint milk; one-half cup sugar; one-fourth cup rolled crackers; one lemon rind.

LEMON CREAM PIE Mrs. Willet Wanzer

Bake the crust, then fill with the following: One cup sugar; one lemon juice and peel; three egg whites saved for frosting; three heaping teaspoonfuls flour stirred up in a little cold water; one teacup boiling water; mix together and boil up. Then place in baked crust. Stir whites of eggs until thick. Add about one-half cup sugar, a little at a time. Then place on pie and brown slightly.

LEMON CREAM PIE Mrs. H. Clay Calhoun

One cupful granulated sugar; one tablespoonful butter, creamed; two tablespoonfuls flour; juice of one large lemon; yolks of two eggs; one cupful milk; stir all together and fold the stiffly beaten whites of the two eggs in last.

LEMON PIE Mrs. R. F. Morrow

One lemon; one-half orange; one cup sugar; yolks three eggs; one cup water; one tablespoonful (heaping) flour; one lump butter; beat all together and cook until thick custard. Put into crust; with whites beat stiff one spoonful sugar.

FLAT CUSTARD PIE Mrs. Earl Combs

Four eggs beaten; one quart of milk; two tablespoonfuls flour; one pinch salt; one tablespoonful butter; put in hot pan. Then pour custard and bake about twenty minutes. When done put creamed sugar on top while hot. Creamed sugar. One cup powdered sugar; two tablespoonfuls butter; one teaspoonful vanilla; cream all together.

CRANBERRY PIE Mrs. Harry M. Boon

One pint cranberries; one-half cup raisins. Wash and cut up raisins, put with cranberries with a small cup of sugar; cook and when soft put in pie crust.

BOSTON CREAM PIE Mrs. J. G. Sherer

Two cups milk; three-fourths cup sugar; three-fourths cup cocoanut; pinch salt. Put in double boiler and heat. Teaspoonful vanilla; three tablespoonfuls corn starch dissolved in a little milk; beaten whites of four eggs last; then beat steadily. Bake crust first. Beat a bottle of cream until stiff; sweeten it with three tablespoonfuls of powdered sugar and a teaspoonful vanilla and spread on pie.

CREAM PIE Mrs. Willet Wanzer

Two egg yolks; four heaping teaspoonfuls sugar; two cups milk; one-half tablespoonful butter; three even tablespoonfuls corn starch; one teaspoonful vanilla. Cook in double boiler until it thickens. Then spread on the baked pie crust, and put the whites beaten with sugar added on top, and brown slightly. To be eaten cold. Chocolate added makes a very delicious pie.

BUTTER SCOTCH PIE Mrs. William Molt

Make and bake crust first, before adding filling. One cup light brown sugar; butter size of an egg; one tablespoonful flour; pinch of salt; mix thoroughly, then add one cup of milk and boil in double boiler until thick; then add beaten yolks of two eggs. Add to the baked crust; beat whites of the two eggs stiff, with a little sugar and brown slightly in oven.

CREAM PIE Mrs. T. M. Butler

One egg, one tablespoonful of flour, three-fourths cup of sugar, butter size of a walnut, one pint of milk. Stir constantly while cooking until thickened and fill previously baked crust and sprinkle over with cocoanut and nutmeg.

BUTTER-SCOTCH PIE Mrs. P. D. Swigart

One and one-half ounces butter; three-fourths cup light brown sugar; two eggs; one and one-half cups sweet milk. Put butter in pan, mix in brown sugar, stirring constantly until caramel color, then add milk and boil until sugar is melted. Separate the yolks from whites, add to yolks one-half cup flour and one teaspoonful corn starch. Add enough water to make a thick paste, stir into ready baked pie crust, put whites to which sugar has been added on top and brown. Instead of whites of egg for top of pie, whipped cream may be substituted.

BUTTER-SCOTCH PIE Mrs. Earl Combs

One-half cup brown sugar; one-half cup white sugar; two yolks of eggs; two tablespoonfuls flour; one large cup milk; two tablespoonfuls butter; dissolve sugar and butter with a small amount of milk; and let boil until it threads a little. Mix flour with a little water to thin paste and then add milk and yolks of eggs. Stir all together and boil until smooth, thick paste. Put in baked crust. Whip whites, put in little sugar, and put on top. Bake a golden brown.

FILLING FOR PUMPKIN PIE Mrs. W. H. Hart

One scant cupful sugar beaten into two eggs; one teaspoonful flour; two heaping tablespoonfuls of cooked pumpkin; spices to suit taste; one and one-half cupfuls of sweet milk. Mix in order given; this makes one large pie. When done and before serving, spread the top with whipped cream; nuts can also be added.

BLUEBERRY PIE Mrs. C. S. Junge

One cup of flour; two heaping tablespoonfuls of lard; three tablespoonfuls of sour cream. Mix lightly into crust. Sprinkle a layer of flour in lower crust and fill with berries. Sprinkle over them two tablespoonfuls of flour and a cup and a half of sugar. Put in two tablespoonfuls of water and add upper crust. Heat stones of cooker fifteen minutes beginning as you begin your pie. Bake pie forty minutes.

SOUR CREAM PIE Mrs. H. Freeman

One cup sour cream; one cup sugar; one-half cup seeded raisins, chopped fine; yolks two eggs; one-half teaspoonful cloves, and cinnamon. Mix one teaspoonful flour with sugar; spread on the pie after it is baked, whites of two eggs beaten to a froth, stiff, with two tablespoonfuls sugar. Set in oven and brown slightly. Cream must be sour.

MOCK CHERRY PIE Belle Shaw

One cup cranberries, split lengthwise (work out seeds); one-half cup raisins chopped fine; one cup sugar with one tablespoonful flour mixed with it. Mix all together; pour in one-half cup boiling water; add one teaspoonful vanilla. Bake between rich crusts.

PUMPKIN PIE Mrs. Max Mauermann

One cup pumpkin; one-fourth cup of sugar; one-half teaspoonful salt; one-fourth teaspoonful cinnamon; one-fourth teaspoonful mace; one-half teaspoonful vanilla; one egg and one yolk, beaten separately, and whites added last; one-half cup milk; one-fourth cup cream; one tablespoonful corn starch. Bake in plain pastry until set.

RICE RAISIN PIE Mrs. C. A. Carscadin

Boil one cup of raisins in one cup of water for five minutes; then add three tablespoonfuls boiled rice and one cup of sugar. Boil another five minutes and add a tablespoonful butter and bake in two crusts.

DUTCH APPLE PIE Mrs. H. Abells

Line pie plate with crust and fill with quartered apples. Add to one cup of sugar, one large tablespoonful of flour and stir into one cup of cream; pour over apples. Grate nutmeg over all and bake without upper crust.

SWEET POTATO PIE Mrs. Earl Combs

One pound of sweet potatoes mashed; two cups of sugar; one cup of cream; one-half cup butter; three eggs well beaten; little nutmeg, pinch of salt. Bake in crust.

SWEET POTATO PIE Mrs. Thomas D. Caliger

Three medium sized potatoes. Boil soft and mash fine. Mix with it yolks of three eggs; sugar, to taste; one tablespoonful butter; flavoring, nutmeg and vanilla to taste. Whip whites of eggs, and add small portion of ground citron.

DESSERTS

"Among the great, whom heaven hath made to shine,
  How few have learned the art of arts,—to dine!"

KISS TORTE Mrs. F. Dunn

Six whites of eggs; two cups granulated sugar; one teaspoonful vinegar; one teaspoonful vanilla. Beat the whites of eggs to a stiff, dry froth; add the sugar a little at a time and beat; add the vanilla and vinegar. Grease a spring form pan and pour in the mixture. Bake about one hour in a slow oven. Serve with crushed strawberries or raspberries and whipped cream. Can be baked in individual molds and the centers filled with berries, etc. Very delicious. Bake forty minutes in a slow oven.

KISS TORTE Mrs. Harry M. Boon

Three egg whites beaten very stiff; gradually put in above one cup of granulated sugar, one teaspoonful vinegar, one-half teaspoonful vanilla. Bake in a very light warm oven in two layers. Fill with one quart ice cream, whip cream on top, use berries if you desire, with cream. Serves four or five people. Recipe can be doubled.

CHERRY TORTE Mrs. H. S. Mount

Thicken cherries with corn starch. Torte: Two tablespoonfuls butter; two tablespoonfuls sugar; one yolk egg. Work little by little into above mixture one cup of flour; put in pie tin and fill with cherries. Bake in oven twenty minutes.

DATE TORTE Mrs. W. F. Barnard

One cupful sugar; three eggs; one cup sliced date; one cup sliced nut meats; three tablespoonfuls flour; one-half teaspoonful salt; one teaspoonful baking powder. Bake about one hour. Serve with whipped cream.

PINEAPPLE CREAM Mrs. C. S. Junge

One cup whipped cream; fifteen marshmallows cut into quarter inch squares; four slices pineapple cut into this mixture and let stand on ice for two hours. Bananas or prunes may be used this same way.

PINEAPPLE BAVARIAN CREAM Mrs. C. S. Junge

One tablespoonful Knox gelatin; one quarter cup cold water; one-half can grated pineapple; one-quarter cup sugar; one-half tablespoonful lemon juice; one and one-half cups whipped cream. Soak gelatin in the cold water. Heat pineapple and add sugar, lemon juice and gelatin. Chill in pan of ice water, stirring constantly. When it begins to thicken, beat until frothy. Fold in cream and turn into molds. When cold serve with maraschino cherry on top.

PINEAPPLE MERINGUE Mrs. May F. Kenfield

Heat one can of grated pineapple and one-half cup granulated sugar and when boiling, thicken with about two tablespoonfuls of corn starch, dissolved in one-fourth cup of water. Boil five minutes. Add juice of one-half lemon and three beaten egg yolks. Remove and cool. Fill pastry shells and cover with a meringue, made of three whites, beaten stiff, with eight tablespoonfuls powdered sugar. Serve very cold.

PINEAPPLE SPONGE

One small fresh pineapple or one and one-half pint can of the fruit; one small cup of sugar; one-half package Knox gelatine; one-halm cup water; whites of four eggs. Soak gelatine two hours in one and one-half cups water. Chop pineapple, put it with juice in a small saucepan with sugar and the remainder of the water. Simmer ten minutes, add gelatine, take from fire immediately and strain (if you prefer to leave the pineapple in, take out before straining) into a basin. When partly cold, add whites of eggs beaten. Beat until mixture begins to thicken. Serve with soft custard, flavored with wine.

WHIPPED CREAM SECRET Mrs. W. H. Muschlet

For one pint whipped cream soak a scant tablespoonful granulated gelatine in enough water, cold, to barely cover, until soft; then add a small half teacupful of boiling water and stir until the gelatine is completely dissolved; after which add three-quarters of a cupful of sugar and flavoring. Turn into a bowl and beat it with an egg beater until it is white, like marshmallows, and begins to become firm. Just as soon as it has reached that point, but before it commences to grow stringy, beat it by spoonfuls into the cream. This will increase the bulk of the latter, and it will keep firm any length of time.

SPANISH CREAM

Pint milk with one-half box Keystone gelatine in double boiler; yolks of two eggs and five tablespoonfuls sugar beaten together very lightly; pour milk, etc., into egg mixture; then return to double boiler and stir constantly. Beat whites of two eggs, pour mixture very gradually with same and stir until cold; then add two tablespoonfuls cream and pour into mold. Stand two hours on ice before serving. Be careful and have mold damp inside, but not wet, before using.

DREAM WHIP Mrs. W. I. Clock

One pint whipping cream; one-half pound marshmallows; two tablespoonfuls sugar; one teaspoonful vanilla; one-fourth pound pecan nuts (other nuts can be substituted if desired). Cut the marshmallows up with scissors, add to stiffly beaten cream; also add sugar and vanilla. Let stand all one day. When ready to serve place a small amount in glasses, adding the chopped nuts, chocolate sauce or any fruit desired. This cream and marshmallow combination can be served as the foundation of any number of desserts.

CHARLOTTE RUSSE Katharine Orr

One-half pint whipping cream; one tablespoonful Keystone white gelatine; one-fourth cup hot water; one-fourth cup powdered sugar; whites of two eggs; flavor with vanilla. Add gelatine when cold to whipped cream and sugar; then flavoring and well beaten whites of eggs. Pour over lady fingers and decorate top with cookies standing up.

DRESDEN CHOCOLATE

One cup stale bread crumbs; one-half grated chocolate; two tablespoonfuls sugar; one-fourth teaspoonful salt. Put in oven in buttered tin until chocolate melts. Serve with whipped cream.

CHOCOLATE LADY FINGER DESSERT Mrs. S. Friedlander

Eighteen large lady fingers divided in half and put in a pan flat side up and pan lined with waxed paper. Melt two cakes Baker's chocolate (sweet) in double boiler with three tablespoonfuls water and two tablespoonfuls sugar. Let cool, then add yolks of four eggs, beating one at a time. Beat four whites stiff and add to above mixture. Take layers of lady fingers, then one of the chocolate mixture, another of lady fingers and so on, making three layers of lady fingers and two of the chocolate mixture. When ready to serve, whip two bottles of cream and put on top. Candied cherries and chopped nuts may be added also.

RIZ AU LAIT Mrs. R. Woods

Boil one-half a cupful of rice in a pint of water until very tender and creamy. Add one cup of milk, a small piece of lemon rind, a handful currants and sugar to taste. Let cook slowly for fifteen minutes and remove from fire. Beat yolk of an egg in a spoonful of milk and stir in the rice; do not set back on fire. Serve cold.

PRUNE SOUFFLE Mrs. William Molt

To one cup stewed prunes, seeded, add three tablespoonfuls sugar; one-half teaspoonful vanilla and beaten whites of three eggs folded in lightly. Steam for two hours in double boiler. (When adding water to boiler be sure it is boiling hot.) Serve hot with whipped cream.

MAPLE CREAM CUSTARD Mrs. Jarvis Weed

Three bottles cream; three eggs beaten very light; one cup pure maple syrup; put all together in a double boiler and stir constantly until very smooth. Line a dish with lady fingers and pour the custard over them; put in ice box and serve when very cold.

PEACH SURPRISE Mrs. W. I. Clock

Canned peaches; maccaroons; whipping cream. Take the juice of peaches and add macaroons broken up. Fill the centers of halves of peaches with this mixture, and serve with whipped cream.

CARAMEL CUSTARD EN SURPRISE Mrs. T. D. McMicken

Caramel custard baked in individual molds. Unmold on rounds of sponge cake a little larger than the custard molds, cover with meringue creamed with almond extract. Sprinkle with sugar and brown. Decorate with blanched almonds on top.

BLUEBERRY SHORTCAKE Mrs. C. A. Jennings

One-half cup butter; one cup sugar; one-half cup milk; two eggs; two and one-half cups flour; two heaping teaspoonfuls baking powder; one pint blueberries. Mix batter and add berries last. Bake in muffin rings or shallow dripping pan. Serve hot.

PEACH SHORTCAKE Mrs. W. N. Hurlbut

Two cups flour; four level teaspoonfuls baking powder; half teaspoonful salt; two teaspoonfuls sugar; one-third cup butter; three-quarters cup milk.

Mix and sift flour, baking powder, salt and sugar, work in butter with finger tips, and add milk gradually. Toss on floured board, divide in two parts, bake in hot oven on large cake tins. Spilt and spread with butter. Sweeten sliced peaches to taste. Crush slightly, and put between and on top of cakes. Cover with whipped cream.

THORN APPLES

Prepare a syrup by boiling eight minutes two cups sugar and three-fourths cup of water. Wipe, core and pare eight apples (Greenings). Drop apples into syrup as soon as pared. Cook slowly until soft but not broken, skim syrup when necessary. Drain from syrup, fill cavities with quince yelly and stick apples thickly with blanched, shredded and delicately toasted almonds. Chill and serve with cream as dessert or use as a garnish with cold meats.

FOOD FOR THE GODS Mrs. J. F. Nichols

One cup sugar; one teaspoonful baking powder; four tablespoonfuls, heaping, cracker crumbs; three eggs, beaten separately; one cup dates; one cup nuts. Bake slowly in oven. Serve with whipped cream.

STRAWBERRY FOAM Mrs. A. J. Langan

One cup strawberries, mashed; one cup sugar; white of one egg beaten stiff; whip all together for ten minutes, serve on pieces of angel food or sunshine cake.

CRUMB TARTAR Mrs. Wm. J. Maiden

One cupful sugar; one cup dates, pitted and chopped; one cupful nuts, chopped; two eggs; one tablespoonful flour; one teaspoonful baking powder; pinch of salt. Mix eggs, sugar and salt, then flour and baking powder, adding the dates and nuts last. Bake in slow oven and serve with whipped cream.

FIGS AS A DESSERT

PUDDINGS

*"The pudding's proof does in the eating lie,
Success is yours, whichever rule you try."*

FIG PUDDING Mrs. C. B. Martin

One cup suet; one cup sugar; one cup milk; one cup of figs, ground; three cups flour; one-half teaspoonful salt; one teaspoonful each of cinnamon and baking powder. Steam two hours.

STEAMED FIG PUDDING Mary Roberts

Three ounces beef suet; one-half ounce figs, chopped fine; two and one-third cups stale bread crumbs; one-half cup milk; two eggs; one cup sugar; three-fourths spoonful salt. Chop suet and work with hands until creamy; then add figs. Soak bread crumbs in milk. Add eggs, well beaten; then sugar and salt. Combine mixture. Steam three hours in a buttered mould. Serve with following sauce:

Sauce: Two eggs; one cup powdered sugar; three tablespoonfuls wine; beat yolks until thick, add one-half of the sugar. Beat whites stiff, add remaining sugar. Combine, and add wine.

FIG PUDDING Mrs. W. K. Mitchell

One cup suet; one cup sugar; one cup milk; three cups flour; one cup figs, ground; two eggs; one-half teaspoonful salt; one teaspoonful each of cinnamon and baking powder. Mix all together and steam about two hours.

CHOCOLATE PUDDING Mrs. C. A. Bowman

One pint of milk; two tablespoonfuls corn starch; one tablespoonful sugar; pinch of salt. Boil until thick, add one heaping teaspoonful cocoa dissolved in a little boiling water, and last the stiffly beaten whites of two eggs. Let all cook one minute and flavor with vanilla.

CHOCOLATE PUDDING Mrs. J. L. Putnam

One pint of milk; one tablespoonful Baker's cocoa; one tablespoonful corn starch; one egg; one and one-half cups sugar. Heat milk in double boiler. Mix dry ingredients and beat in egg. Add to scalded milk. Boil fifteen minutes. Remove from fire and whip with egg beater. Add one teaspoonful vanilla. Serve with cream.

STEAMED CHOCOLATE PUDDING Mrs. William H. Fahrney

One and one-half tablespoonfuls butter; two-thirds cup sugar; one egg; one cup milk; one-half teaspoonful salt; two and one-fourth cups flour; three teaspoonfuls baking powder; two squares of chocolate, melted. Steam in a buttered pudding mold, tightly covered, for two hours.

Cream Sauce: One-fourth cup butter; one cup powdered sugar; stir until creamy; then add one cup whipped cream just before serving; flavor.

STEAMED CHOCOLATE PUDDING Mrs. H. R. Foster

Three-fourths cup sugar; one tablespoon butter, creamed. Two eggs; one-half cup milk; one and one-half cups sifted flour; one and one-half teaspoonfuls baking powder; two squares melted chocolate, or two tablespoonfuls cocoa; one teaspoonful vanilla. Steam one hour and serve with hard sauce.

CHOCOLATE ICE-BOX PUDDING

Two cakes sweet chocolate; two tablespoonfuls boiling water; one-fourth cup confectioner's sugar; yolks four eggs; whites four eggs; nut meats; lady fingers. Melt chocolate in top of double boiler; remove from range, add boiling water and the yolks of eggs beaten until thick and light. Fold in the stiffly beaten whites of eggs. Line a small pan (dimensions, 7-1/2 x 4-3/4 x 2-1/2) with wax paper. Put in a layer of split lady fingers cut to fit and cover bottom; cover these with half of the chocolate mixture; sprinkle with bits of trimmings of lady fingers and nut meats. Cover with a layer of lady fingers, pour over remainder of chocolate mixture, sprinkle with nut meats and chill in refrigerator twenty-four hours. Serve with whipped cream.

CARAMEL PUDDING Mrs. H. R. Foster

One-half pint brown sugar; one-half pint cold water; one-fourth box gelatine; four eggs, whites; one-half teaspoonful vanilla. Soak gelatine in one gill of cold water. Put sugar and other gill of water in saucepan and boil until it becomes a thick syrup. Add gelatine and vanilla and again heat to boiling point. Beat whites to stiff froth. Pour hot syrup on eggs, beating until cold. Turn into mold and serve on flat dish with custard sauce made from yolks of eggs.

MOLASSES PUDDING Mrs. C. A. Carscadin

One egg well beaten; two tablespoonfuls sugar, rounded; one tablespoonful butter, level; one pinch salt; one-half cup molasses; one and one-half cups flour, well sifted; one teaspoonful baking powder; one teaspoonful soda, level, dissolved in one-half cup boiling water. Steam in buttered tins two hours.

Sauce: Two eggs; one-half cup sugar; pinch salt; half teaspoonful vanilla; cream together and add one cup of whipped cream.

ICE-BOX PUDDING Katherine T. Peck

Scant one-fourth cup unsalted butter; one cup granulated sugar; cream together. Add yolks of three eggs, one at a time, rind of one lemon, half; and juice of one lemon. Beat the whites of the three eggs and add last. Place mixture alternately with lady fingers, three dozen lady fingers will serve eight people. Put oil paper in bottom of dish to lift pudding out easily. Serve with whipped cream. Place in ice-box until thoroughly chilled. Can be made the night before.

ICE BOX CAKE Mrs. J. F. Nichols

One dozen lady fingers; one tablespoonful sugar; three eggs, separated; one cake sweet chocolate. Melt chocolate in double boiler with tablespoonful warm water. Add mixture of yolks of eggs and sugar, well beaten, a little vanilla, and lastly well-beaten whites of eggs. Dip each lady finger in mixture, arrange in form which has been wet with cold water, and fill in. Place in ice box over night. Serve with whipped cream.

ICE BOX CAKE Mrs. H. S. Mount

Three cakes sweet chocolate, three tablespoonfuls powdered sugar, three tablespoonfuls hot water, two dozen lady fingers. Melt chocolate, sugar and water in double boiler and add half beaten yolks of six eggs. Cook until thick. When cold add beaten whites of six eggs. Line a mold with lady fingers and pour half the mixture on them, then fill with lady fingers, repeating with the chocolate mixture. Made twenty-four hours before served. Just before serving, whip one-half pint cream and put on top of cake. Grate a little chocolate over all.

SPONGE PUDDING Mrs. C. A. Carscadin

One-fourth cup sugar; one-half cup flour; one pint milk; one-fourth cup butter; five eggs. Mix sugar and flour, and add milk and cook until thick and smooth. Let cool, then add butter. Separate eggs, beat yolks until light and fold into mixture. Add whites beaten stiff, and pour into buttered dish. Stand dish in pan of water and bake in moderate oven one-half hour.

Sauce: One-fourth cup butter; one-half cup powdered sugar; four tablespoonfuls cream added slowly, one teaspoonful vanilla. Set mixture over pan of boiling water until creamy.

SUNSHINE PUDDING Mrs. Carscadin

One-half cup flour; one-fourth cup sugar; one-fourth butter; one pint milk; five eggs. Mix sugar and flour; add milk; and cook until smooth in double boiler. Take off stove and add butter. Separate eggs, beat yolks and add. Beat whites until stiff and add. Butter pan, set in pan of water and bake.

Sauce: One-fourth cup butter; one-half cup powdered sugar; four tablespoonfuls cream, added slowly.

DATE PUDDING Mrs. W. I. Clock

One cupful sugar; one cupful chopped nut meats; one cupful dates; two eggs; one-half cupful milk; one tablespoonful flour and one teaspoonful baking powder. Bake twenty or thirty minutes in moderate oven. When baking the pudding raises beautifully, but when done it falls in the center; this is the correct occurrence.

PEACH PUDDING Mrs. E. Oliver

Butter pudding dish. Slice six large peaches in it. Batter: One cup sugar; one egg; one and one-half teaspoonfuls baking powder; butter size of an egg; three tablespoonfuls of milk; flour enough to make a soft batter. Pour over peaches and bake twenty minutes. Serve hot, with cream.

CREAM PUDDING

One cup nut meats; one cup dates; cut very coarse. One tablespoonful bread crumbs; one cup sugar; two eggs, beaten separately; add whites last. Bake twenty minutes in slow oven. Serve cold with whipped cream.

SOUR CREAM PUDDING Mrs. William H. Fahrney

One cup brown sugar; two eggs; pinch of salt; one cup sour cream; one teaspoonful soda; two cups flour; three-fourths cup nuts. Bake.

Sauce: Cream one cup powdered sugar and one-fourth cup butter; add one egg; one teaspoonful vanilla or tablespoonful sherry wine.

APPLE PUDDING Miss Flora Gill

One cup sugar; one cup flour; two eggs; one-half cup of sweet milk; fill a three-pint baking dish with sliced apples, two-thirds full. Add one-half cup of sugar, a little cinnamon, and some water. Bake until very tender. When still very hot pour over the top a cake batter made as follows: Beat one cup of sugar with yolks of two eggs; one tablespoonful soft butter, and milk and flour. Mix two heaping teaspoonfuls of baking powder with flour before adding to the batter. Fold in stiffly beaten whites of the eggs and add extract of vanilla. Bake half an hour in a moderate oven. Serve with prepared sauce.

LEMON PUDDING Mrs. W. I. Clock

Mix three tablespoonfuls corn starch; three cups boiling water; two cups sugar; two egg yolks; juice of two lemons, little grated rind of one. Dissolve three tablespoonfuls of corn starch in a little cold water, add to the boiling water. Have saucepan in water bath. Add sugar and lemons, cook for twenty minutes. Remove from fire and stir in beaten egg yolks; set mixture in oven for two minutes and serve with cream.

SOUR MILK BLUEBERRY PUDDING Mrs. C. S. Junge

One-half cup sugar; one-quarter cup butter; cream these. Two eggs well beaten; one-half cup sour milk; one-half teaspoonful soda; one cup flour with one cup blueberries. Bake thirty minutes and serve with sauce made with one cup of powdered sugar stirred with one tablespoonful of butter and flavored with vanilla.

CARROT PUDDING Mrs. P. D. Swigart

One and one-half cups flour; one cup sugar; one cup suet; two cups raisins; one cup grated sweet potatoes; one cup grated carrots; one teaspoonful each salt and soda. Steam three hours; put three tablespoonfuls hot water on soda.

Sauce: Two yolks of eggs; one cup powdered sugar; cream the above. Last thing, add a cup whipped cream.

CARROT PUDDING Mrs. Frederick T. Hoyt

One cup chopped raw carrots; one cup chopped raw potatoes; one cup chopped suet; two cups chopped raisins; one cup brown sugar; one cup flour; one teaspoonful salt, cinnamon and allspice; a little nutmeg; one teaspoonful soda in about two tablespoonfuls hot water. Mix well, put in mold, and steam two and one-half hours; serve with a good pudding sauce.

Pudding Sauce: One cup sugar; two egg yolks; one cup sherry wine; beat all until very light, add one pint cream, which has been whipped very stiff.

PRUNE PUDDING Mrs. Eustace

Whites of five eggs beaten with one-half teaspoonful of salt; add one cup of powdered sugar sifted with one even teaspoonful cream of tartar. Add five large cooked prunes chopped. Bake twenty-two minutes in ungreased custard cups. Set in pan of hot water. Slow oven. Serve with whipped cream.

STEAMED MARMALADE PUDDING Mrs. T. D. McMicken

One cup orange marmalade; one-fourth cup butter; one-third teaspoonful soda; two cups stale bread crumbs. Dissolve soda in a little hot water; combine marmalade, one egg, butter, soda, and bread crumbs. Pack in a mold. Steam one and one-half hours. Serve with marshmallow cream.

GRAHAM PUDDING Mrs. R. H. Wheeler

One cup molasses; one cup sweet milk; two and one-half cups graham flour; one cup Sultana raisins; one saltspoonful salt; two teaspoonfuls soda dissolved in warm water. Steam in pudding mold two hours.

Sauce: One egg thoroughly beaten. Add one cup pulverized sugar; one cup whipped cream; one-half teaspoonful vanilla.

BROWN BETTY

Butter the inside of a baking dish, cover the bottom with a layer of tart apples, peeled and sliced. Sprinkle this with sugar and cinnamon or nutmeg and put over it a layer of crumbs, strewing it with bits of butter. Repeat the layers of apple and crumbs until the dish is full, making the top crumbs with an extra quantity of butter. Cover the pudding dish, put it in the oven, and bake slowly for twenty or thirty minutes; uncover, brown lightly; serve in the dish in which it was cooked, with either hard or liquid sauce.

SURPRISE PUDDING Mrs. C. E. Upham

Four thin slices bread, buttered and cut in squares; one egg; one-third cup sugar; four tablespoonfuls molasses; three cups milk; turn all over bread. Let stand half an hour and mash well together; then bake one and one-half hours slowly. Be careful it does not turn to whey. If in a shallow pan, a big hour is long enough. Sauce: Beat white of one egg, then beat yolk; mix, add one cupful sugar, vanilla, and beat all together. Beating separately makes it very frothy.

CHERRY PUDDING Mrs. P. D. Swigart

One-half cup sugar; one tablespoonful butter; one egg; one-half cup milk or water; one and one-half cups flour; one and one-half teaspoonfuls baking powder. Steam forty minutes, put cherries in cups, then the batter.

Sauce: One and one-half cups cherry juice; one tablespoonful butter; sweeten; thicken with corn starch.

SIMPLE HASTY FRUIT PUDDING Mrs. C. S. Junge

One tablespoonful butter; two tablespoonfuls sugar; three tablespoonfuls flour; one teaspoonful baking powder; two tablespoonfuls milk; one egg. Turn this mixture over sliced peaches, bananas, oranges, blueberries, pineapples or plums and bake twenty minutes in moderate oven. Serve with cream or with hard sauce made by rubbing butter and sugar together.

ECONOMICAL PUDDING Mrs. Minnie A. Watkins

Fill a mold with dry pieces of cake, alternating layers with bananas that have been scraped and cut lengthwise. Fill up mold with a boiled custard thickened with yolks of eggs. Put on ice. Serve cold with whipped cream. Also serve toasted Brazilian nut meats with it.

PHILADELPHIA RICE PUDDING Mrs. B. Z. Bisbee

Wash well one-fourth cup of rice. Put in a baking dish with one quart of milk, four tablespoonfuls of sugar, lump of butter size of a walnut; flavor to taste with nutmeg and cinnamon. Bake in a very slow oven four hours; when it commences to brown on top stir well. Serve cold.

NOONDAY DESSERT FOR SCHOOL CHILDREN Mrs. Minnie A. Watkins

Hot steamed rice served with rich canned peaches, and cream, either plain or whipped. Serve English walnut meats with same.

MOTHER'S RICE PUDDING Mrs. F. E. Lyons

One quart milk; three tablespoonfuls rice; three tablespoonfuls sugar; one teaspoonful vanilla. Put in a very slow oven and bake from two and one-half hours to three hours. (If heated on top of stove before putting in oven, it will save time baking.)

HONEYCOMB PUDDING Mrs. C. A. Bowman

One-half cup brown sugar; one-half cup milk; one cup molasses; one teaspoonful soda; two eggs; tablespoonful butter; one cup flour. Bake and serve with whipped cream or hard sauce.

INDIVIDUAL PUDDINGS Miss Nora Edmonds

One-half cupful flour; one-fourth cupful sugar; one-fourth cupful butter; one pint of milk and five eggs. Mix flour and sugar, add milk and cook in double boiler until smooth. Remove from stove and put in butter. When cold add beaten yolks of eggs and fold in stiffly beaten whites last. Put in buttered pans and bake in water.

Sauce: One-fourth cupful butter; one-half cupful powdered sugar and four tablespoonfuls cream added.

TAPIOCA CREAM Mrs. A. H. Schweizer

Soak one tablespoonful of pearl tapioca until soft in enough water to cover it. This will require several hours. Put it into a double boiler with a cupful of water and cook until the pearls are clear; drain off the water and stir in half a pint of grape juice heated, one tablespoonful sugar, and cook ten minutes longer. Serve with cream when cold.

ENGLISH PUDDING Mrs. William Molt

One-half pound suet; one quart milk; two eggs; one pound currants; one pound raisins; one cup nut meats, chopped fine; two teaspoonfuls baking powder; one teaspoonful salt and flour enough to make a stiff batter. Steam for four to five hours. Serve with foam sauce.

Foam Sauce: White of one egg; enough confectionery sugar to make stiff and enough hot water to make it smooth.

ORANGE PUDDING Mrs. H. B. Rairden

In bottom of pudding dish lay slices of cake; cover with slices of oranges. Make a custard of one small cup sugar; one tablespoonful corn starch; one pint of milk and a small piece of butter. Pour over the cake and oranges and bake.

ENGLISH PUDDING Miss J. Eliza Ball

One cup molasses; one-half cup sugar; one-half cup butter; two eggs; one cup milk. Spice and fruit. Flour enough to make a stiff batter. Soda and cream of tartar or baking powder as preferred.

Liquid Pudding Sauce: Beat one egg and one cup of white sugar to a froth. Make a very thin batter with one pint of water and butter the size of an egg. Pour butter boiling hot over egg and sugar just as it goes to the table.

CHRISTMAS PUDDING Mrs. Joel H. Norton

Chop the meats from one pound English walnuts; chop one pound figs; one pound raisins seeded; one cup suet. Rub the above well in flour; grate one nutmeg into three cups flour and one teaspoonful salt. Moisten with one cup milk. Dissolve well one teaspoonful soda in one cup molasses, and add last with one tablespoonful brandy. Dip a square of cloth in boiling water; then quickly flour center. Mold in form of a ball and tie securely with string. Boil three or four hours in boiling water in very large kettle or boiler. Hang up to dry and when thoroughly dry place in jar with an apple to keep from molding. Make a week or two before you wish to use it. Boil it in boiling hot water for one hour when ready to use. Any sauce will do, but whipped cream sweetened with maple sugar is delicious. Brandy can be poured over pudding and set on fire if you wish, if served at table.

NUT PUDDING Mrs. R. E. P. Kline

Two cups flour; one-half cup sugar; two teaspoonfuls baking powder; one-half teaspoonful salt; two eggs well beaten; one cup milk; one and one-half cups English walnuts blanched and broken or chopped; one-third cup melted butter. Grease mold well and steam three hours.

Sauce: One and one-half cups sugar and three-fourths cup water boiled until it threads. Then pour over the well beaten yolks of three eggs, stirring all the time. When cool, add flavoring and two cups whipped cream.

NUT PUDDING Miss Julia Hunt

Two cups boiling water; one and three-fourths cups brown sugar, boil ten minutes. Two and one-half tablespoonfuls (heaping) corn starch mixed well with one-third cup cold water; add to boiling syrup; boil a few minutes until mixture thickens, then add one-half cup broken walnut meats and vanilla.

Pour into molds and chill. Raisins and currants may be added if desired. Serve with cream or whipped cream.

PUDDING SAUCE Mrs. R. F. Morrow

One cup brown sugar; one-fourth cup butter; yolks of two eggs; one-half cup cream; cook to a custard. Add beaten whites, and one-fourth cup brandy.

PUDDING SAUCE Mrs. Weatherell

Blend one tablespoonful butter, one cup sugar and white of one egg (do not beat egg separately). Dissolve one tablespoonful corn starch and a little salt and add to one pint of boiling water. Let cook ten minutes. Then add the butter, egg and sugar, and whip until foamy. Flavor to taste.

PUDDING SAUCE Mrs. H. D. Sheldon

Two eggs; one cup powdered sugar; one cup cream; a pinch of salt. Beat eggs and gradually add sugar until a smooth creamy consistency. Just before serving add whipped cream.

FRUIT SAUCE Mrs. May F. Kenfield

For steamed or baked puddings: One-half cup of butter and one and one-half cups of powdered sugar; cream together and add yolk of one egg. Then to this add a cupful of crushed strawberries or any fruit in season.

HARD SAUCE Mrs. W. D. Hurlbut

Four tablespoonfuls butter; eight of powdered sugar; frothed white of one egg; half a glass of wine. Cream butter and sugar together; add wine, then white of the egg. Set in a cool place to harden. Grate nutmeg over top.

www.ingramcontent.com/pod-product-compliance
Lightning Source LLC
Chambersburg PA
CBHW081622100526
44590CB00021B/3558